The
Illustrated
Encyclopedia
of
Animals

**An Incredible Journey
Through the Animal Kingdom**

written by
Claudia Martin

illustrated by
Marc Pattenden

ARCTURUS

ARCTURUS

This edition published in 2023 by Arcturus Publishing Limited
26/27 Bickels Yard, 151–153 Bermondsey Street, London SE1 3HA

Author: Claudia Martin
Illustrator: Marc Pattenden
Designer: Suzanne Cooper
Consultant: Jules Howard
Editor: Becca Clunes
Design Manager: Jessica Holliland
Editorial Manager: Joe Harris

ISBN: 978-1-3988-2571-0
CH010463NT
Supplier 29, Date 0523, Print run 00003457

Printed in China

Contents

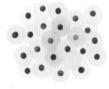

Amazing Animals

Amazing animals live in all our planet's habitats, from rain forests to deserts and cities to coral reefs. Scientists estimate that there are at least 20 quintillion (2 followed by 19 zeros) animals alive today. These animals belong to more than 1.5 million different species. Among the most common species are tiny ocean-living animals such as the Antarctic krill, which numbers in at least the trillions. Among the rarest species are the many animals at risk of extinction, such as the Bornean orangutan and red wolf. These animals have been endangered by—and can be protected by—the activities of the planet's smartest species: humans.

Around two-thirds of animals are meat-eaters, feeding on other animals—from insects to fish and mammals—at least part of the time. The world's deadliest killer is probably the largest animal of all, the 29.9-m (98-ft) long blue whale. It feeds on krill, consuming around 40 million in a single day and as many as 1 trillion in its 80-year life. The remaining third of animals feed on plants or living things such as seaweed or mushrooms. The world's biggest land animal, the 3.96-m (13-ft) tall African bush elephant, is a plant-eater. The elephant's great size protects it from predators and—since it has no need to run fast, hide, or leap to catch prey—does not prevent it from finding food.

Many insects, from bees to fruit flies, live for only the time taken to mature, mate, and lay eggs, which may be as little as 50 days. Yet many larger animals live for years, decades, or even centuries. Perhaps the longest lived is the slow-swimming, slow-growing Greenland shark, which may survive for up to 500 years. A tiny jellyfish, known as the immortal jellyfish, could live for longer, as it can regenerate itself by changing back into its immature form when it is old or sick. Yet it is likely to be eaten by a predator long before it reaches 500 years old. Like all the world's amazing animals, large and small, it is locked in a constant battle to feed, mate, and survive another day.

A close relative of humans, the Bornean orangutan is endangered by hunting and the cutting down of trees in its rain forest habitat.

Found in African grasslands
and forests, the African bush
elephant lives for 60 to 70 years,
while the smaller giraffe and
zebra live for around 25 years.

Animal Groups

Animals share some key characteristics. All animals must feed on other living things. They need the gas oxygen, which is used as fuel for turning food into energy. Animals must also take in water, which transports materials around the body. During at least part of an animal's life, it can move.

Scientists have divided animals into six groups, based on their shared characteristics: fish, amphibians, reptiles, birds, mammals, and invertebrates. Within these groups, animals are divided into smaller and smaller groups of more and more similar animals, such as classes, orders, families, and species.

A species is a group of animals that look and behave alike and can mate together to produce young. For example, humans are a species with the scientific name *Homo sapiens* (meaning "wise human" in Latin). Humans are in the family of great apes, in the order of primates, in the class of mammals.

BIRDS

Birds have a lightweight skeleton, feathers, and wings. Most, but not all, birds can fly. Birds have a toothless beak made of bone and keratin, the same material found in feathers, claws, scales, and hair. They have lungs for breathing air and lay hard-shelled eggs on land.

AMPHIBIANS

Amphibians usually hatch from a jelly-like egg in fresh water, where they soak up oxygen using gills. After going through changes known as metamorphosis, most amphibians develop lungs for taking oxygen from air and start to live on land. Amphibians have thin skin protected by a slippery liquid called mucus.

FISH

Fish are water-living animals that soak up oxygen from water using body parts called gills. Their skin is usually protected by small, hard plates called scales. Most fish have body parts called fins, which help with swimming. The majority of fish lay jelly-like eggs in water, but a few give birth to live babies.

REPTILES

Reptiles have lungs for breathing air. Some live in water but swim regularly to the surface to breathe. They have skin protected by scales or by larger, bonier plates called scutes. Most reptiles lay tough-shelled eggs on land, but some give birth to live young.

MAMMALS

Mammals grow hair during at least part of their life. Nearly all give birth to live young, which they feed on milk. Mammals have lungs, so those that live in water return to the surface to breathe air. Mammals usually have four limbs, which may be adapted to walking, jumping, climbing, flying, or swimming.

INVERTEBRATES

Invertebrates—which make up 97 percent of all animals—do not have a backbone. They have many different body types and methods of taking oxygen from air or water. Common groups include insects such as butterflies and beetles, which have a hard covering, a three-part body, and six legs; cnidarians such as jellyfish and corals, which have stinging tentacles; and mollusks such as octopus and snails, which have a soft body that may be covered by a shell.

Habitats

A habitat is the natural home of an animal, plant, or other living thing. Habitats can be vast or tiny, ranging from a wide rain forest to the bark of a kapok tree in that forest. Every animal is suited to finding food, water, and shelter in the habitat where it lives.

LAND BIOMES

A biome is a vast habitat: a wide region that is home to a particular group of animals and plants. Different regions have different biomes because of their climate, which is their usual weather. Areas close to the equator are hotter and wetter than areas around the poles.

Different types of plants grow in different climates—or if it is very cold or dry, they cannot grow at all. Plants provide food and shelter for animals. The animals in a biome have a body and habits suited to the biome's level of heat, light, water, and shelter.

This map shows the world's major land biomes.

POLAR ICE	An icy, dry biome where plants cannot grow.	
TUNDRA	A cold, dry biome where only low plants can grow.	
CONIFEROUS FOREST	A biome with long, cold winters where many conifer trees grow.	
MOUNTAINS	A biome that is colder and windier than the surrounding region.	
TEMPERATE FOREST	A biome with moderate rainfall and temperatures where many trees grow.	

GRASSLAND	A biome with low rainfall where most plants are grasses.
SHRUBLAND	A warm, fairly dry, often windy biome where most plants are shrubs.
DESERT	A biome with very low rainfall and extreme temperatures where few plants can grow.
RAIN FOREST	A biome with heavy rainfall where trees grow thickly.

MICROHABITATS

Every biome contains microhabitats. These are very small habitats with different conditions from their biome. For example, fallen leaves create a microhabitat with darker and wetter conditions than the temperate forest biome they are in. The earwigs and spiders in this microhabitat are suited to its conditions. Microhabitats include a rotting log, the underside of a rock in a stream, and a tidal pool on the seashore.

The rain that collects in a bromeliad in the Amazon rain forest creates a microhabitat. This is an essential habitat for the tadpoles of the Amazon poison dart frog.

WATER BIOMES

Around 70 percent of Earth's surface is covered by water. The marine biome consists of all Earth's salty water, which flows in oceans and seas. This biome has many smaller habitats, which receive different amounts of light and warmth from the Sun. These habitats include sunlit, warm coral reefs and deep, dark, cold waters. The freshwater biome is made up of the 3 percent of Earth's water that does not contain salt. Freshwater habitats include rivers, lakes, and wetlands. The range of animals, plants, and other living things in these habitats depends on the water temperature, depth, and flow.

Covering less than 1 percent of the ocean floor, coral reefs are home to 25 percent of ocean animals. Reefs are one of Earth's most biodiverse habitats, which means they have a high number of different species.

Polar Ice

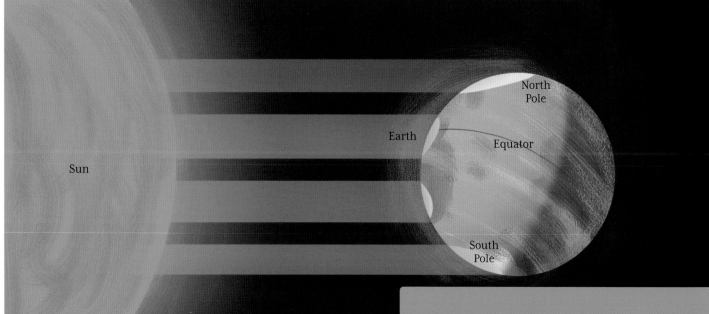

The Sun's rays strike Earth most directly near the equator. At the poles, the same amount of heat is spread out over a larger area, making polar regions much colder than equatorial regions.

The polar biome is in Earth's far north and south, around the poles. The North Pole is in the Arctic Ocean, where the world's largest island, Greenland, lies in the polar zone. The South Pole is in the middle of the continent of Antarctica, which is also in the polar zone. In the polar biome, around 99 percent of the land is covered by ice, where plants cannot grow. Part of the Arctic Ocean, as well as the Southern Ocean around Antarctica, is also always covered by ice.

At the South Pole, the average winter air temperature is -60 °C (-76 °F). At the North Pole, it is -40 °C (-40 °F). The North Pole is warmer than the South Pole because it is warmed by the ocean, which never drops below -2 °C (28 °F). The poles are cold because, when the Sun appears above the horizon there, it is always low in the sky. This is because the Sun is roughly overhead at the equator as Earth circles our star.

At the poles, the Sun's rays hit Earth at an angle, giving less warmth. However, Earth orbits the Sun on a tilt. When the North Pole is tilted toward the Sun, it has its summer, and the Sun never fully sets for six months. When the North Pole is tilted away from the Sun, it has winter, and the Sun does not appear fully above the horizon. When the North Pole has its winter, the South Pole has its summer.

Emperor penguin of Antarctica

The polar land biome is home to few animals due to the cold and lack of plants for food and shelter. However, some animals are found along the coasts of the Arctic and Southern Oceans and on the sea ice, where many feed in the ocean. All polar animals have characteristics that help them survive the extreme cold, such as thick layers of fur, feathers, or fat. Some polar animals visit only in summer, moving out to sea or to warmer regions in winter.

Antarctica's coast is visited by hardy animals such as Weddell seals and southern giant petrels. Six species of seals rest or give birth on the Antarctic coast, surrounding islands, or sea ice. Around 46 seabird species nest on Antarctica. The only other animals on the continent are a few invertebrates, including the flightless Antarctic midge, the largest fully land-living animal at just 6 mm (0.2 in) long.

Arctic Sea Ice

In winter, when the air temperature can drop to -69 °C (-93 °F), ice covers most of the Arctic Ocean, around 15 million sq km (5.8 million sq miles). Much of the sea ice melts in spring and summer, shrinking to around 4 million sq km (1.5 million sq miles).

Up to 20 m (65.6 ft) thick, sea ice provides resting places for seals and walruses. These ocean-living mammals, which must breathe oxygen from air, also give birth on the ice. Hunting seabirds perch on the sea ice, while even a few land-living mammals venture there in search of food.

Global warming has shrunk the Arctic sea ice: In summer, it is around 13 percent smaller than 10 years ago. This has increased the distance that animals must swim to reach resting, feeding, and birthing spots, as well as cutting off migration routes for land-living mammals.

WALRUS

The walrus has four flippers and a streamlined body suited to swimming. It spends much of its time resting on the ice between dives in search of clams, snails, and worms. The walrus uses its tusks, which are extra-long teeth, for climbing onto the slippery ice and making holes in it.

NARWHAL

The narwhal is a whale, a mammal that spends its entire life in water. In winter, the narwhal dives for fish beneath the ice. Every 25 minutes, it surfaces to breathe at a crack. Male narwhals and a few females have a tusk, up to 3.1 m (10.2 ft) long, which males probably use to attract females.

PEARY CARIBOU

This deer lives on the islands of the Canadian Arctic. It uses sea ice as a bridge between its winter and summer feeding grounds on different islands. These movements also let caribou from different islands mate with each other, so the population stays large and healthy.

IVORY GULL

During winter, this seabird lives near a polynya, an area of open ocean water surrounded by sea ice. It seizes fish from the water, but also follows polar bears to feed on their leftovers.

ARCTIC FOX

This fox has thick fur, which also covers the pads of its feet. Its body is compact, while its ears and legs are short, so it has less surface from which to lose body heat. In winter, it follows polar bears over the sea ice, so it can eat the remains of their kills.

HARP SEAL

A female harp seal gives birth to one pup each February. An adult has silver and black fur, but a newborn's fur is white for camouflage on the sea ice. A mother feeds her pup on milk for 12 days before returning to the water to hunt. The pup must survive on its stored body fat until it can hunt, at 4 weeks old.

Polar Bear

The world's largest land-living meat-eater, a polar bear can weigh as much as 700 kg (1,500 lb)— more than eight adult men. Although polar bears are usually born on land, they spend most of their life on the Arctic sea ice, where they hunt for seals.

SEAL HUNTER

The polar bear uses its powerful sense of smell to find the holes in sea ice where seals come up for air or to rest. The bear waits nearby, barely moving for perhaps several hours, as it waits for a seal to appear. Then the bear uses a front paw, which is armed with sharp claws, to drag the seal onto the ice. The bear kills with its strong jaws, which have 42 jagged-edged teeth.

A polar bear is well suited to its life on the sea ice. Its paws are up to 30 cm (12 in) wide, spreading the bear's weight so the ice does not crack as it walks. The paws are also effective paddles when the bear swims between ice floes. The bear is kept warm by a 10-cm- (4-in-) thick layer of body fat, as well as long, pale fur that acts as camouflage.

Polar bears often prey on ringed seals, as well as harp, common, hooded, and bearded seals. After eating, a polar bear washes itself with water or snow.

Mother polar bears are protective of their cubs, fighting off predators such as male bears. Mothers make a chuffing noise when young cubs wander too far away.

BEAR CUBS

Adult polar bears usually live alone, but males and females meet at seal resting spots during the mating season. After mating, the female eats extra food so that she gains fat. When preparing to give birth, she usually goes ashore, where she digs a den in a snowdrift. A narrow entrance tunnel leads to a chamber where, protected from cold and wind, she normally gives birth to two cubs.

For the first 3 months, mother and cubs stay in their den. Toothless and helpless, the cubs are fed on their mother's milk while she lives off her stored fat. When the pups weigh at least 10 kg (22 lb), their mother leads them to the sea ice, where she hunts for food for them all. The cubs learn to hunt by copying their mother. After around 2.5 years, cubs are left to care for themselves.

Polar Bear Facts

SPECIES *Ursus maritimus*

FAMILY Bears

CLASS Mammals

SIZE 1.8–3 m (5.9–9.8 ft) long

RANGE Arctic Ocean and northern coasts of North America, Europe, and Asia

DIET Seals as well as walruses, musk oxen, fish, birds, eggs, and plants

Penguins

Penguins have flipper-shaped wings that are suited to swimming but useless for flight.
There are 18 penguin species, all found in the southern hemisphere apart
from the Galápagos penguin, which lives on the equator. Six species spend
part of their life on Antarctica or nearby islands.

GENTOO PENGUIN

The gentoo is the fastest-swimming penguin, reaching 36 km/h (22 miles per hour) as it dives for small invertebrates called krill. Like all penguins, the gentoo spends three-quarters of its life at sea, but returns to land to nest. Females lay two eggs among grass on the northernmost portion of Antarctica, known as the Antarctic Peninsula, or on islands around Antarctica.

ADÉLIE PENGUIN

During the long Antarctic winter, Adélies stay at sea, where temperatures are a little warmer. At the start of summer, in late October, they return to the Antarctic coast to build nests from stones. Females lay two eggs, which both parents take turns sitting on to keep them warm.

CHINSTRAP PENGUIN

The chinstrap is named for the black line in the feathers across its throat. Like other penguins, the chinstrap has an upright stance on land, waddling slowly on its short legs and webbed feet. To move faster across snow, chinstraps slide on their belly while pushing with their feet.

MACARONI PENGUIN

Like all penguins, the macaroni has a form of camouflage known as countershading: Its belly is white, while its back and flippers are black. When swimming, the penguin's pale belly is difficult to spot against the sunlit water by a predator or prey swimming below. Viewed from above, the penguin's black back blends into the dark depths.

Penguin Facts

FAMILY	Penguins
CLASS	Birds
SIZE	0.3–1.1 m (1–3.6 ft) tall
RANGE	Coastal oceans and coasts of the southern hemisphere
DIET	Fish, krill, and squid

EMPEROR PENGUIN

The only penguin that lays eggs during the Antarctic winter, when temperatures fall to -40 °C (-40 °F), the emperor has thick layers of fat and feathers to keep warm. After a female lays her single egg, her mate balances it on his feet, warming it under skin and feathers.

KING PENGUIN

The second largest penguin after the emperor, the king is up to 1 m (3.3 ft) tall. King penguin chicks move into groups called crèches when they are a few weeks old. In a crèche, chicks huddle together for warmth, watched over by a few adults. Their parents hunt at sea, returning regularly with food.

Tundra

Soil that thaws
in summer

Permafrost

Unfrozen soil

In tundra regions, a permanently frozen layer of soil, called permafrost, lies beneath the ground. In summer, ice in the topmost layer of soil melts, but the permafrost stays below 0 °C (32 °F). The permafrost may extend to 680 m (2,230 ft) below the soil surface.

The word "tundra" comes from the Finnish word *tunturia*, which means "treeless plain." Tundra is a cold, dry biome that lies between the polar and coniferous forest biomes. Most of the world's tundra is in the far north, in a narrow band across northern Asia, Europe, and North America. Islands close to Antarctica are also in the tundra zone. In addition, areas of alpine tundra are on the slopes of high mountains, between the snow-covered peaks and the forests below.

In the tundra biome, no month has an average temperature higher than 10 °C (50 °F), but at least one month is warm enough to melt snow. However, a layer of soil, known as permafrost, remains frozen all year. When the snow melts in summer, the water cannot drain through the permafrost, leaving the ground marshy. There is little rain or snowfall because cold air cannot hold much moisture. No trees are found on the tundra due to the low temperatures and short summer growing season. Trees have deep roots, which cannot reach through the frozen soil. However, the tundra is home to tough, low plants such as grasses, mosses, and shrubs.

Tundra animals must withstand the cold and produce their young during the brief summer. There are very few amphibians and reptiles on the tundra, since these animals are "cold-blooded," which means they cannot

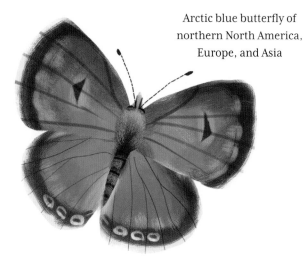

Arctic blue butterfly of northern North America, Europe, and Asia

make their own body heat. However, there are mammals large and small, usually kept warm by thick fat or fur. Some mammals migrate to warmer regions in winter, while many hibernate by resting in a burrow. In the summer, the tundra sees the arrival of countless birds, which nest here while feeding on the rich plant and insect life that warmer temperatures bring.

On Russia's Kola Peninsula, meat-eating mammals include the wolverine and brown bear. Although both also feed on berries, roots, and seeds, they will be glad to catch a rock ptarmigan, one of the few birds that stays on the tundra throughout the year. The ptarmigan's plumage changes so that it remains camouflaged in the changing landscape: Its feathers are white in winter but brown and white in spring or summer.

Canadian Tundra

Canada has around 1.4 million sq km (550,000 sq miles) of Arctic tundra, much of it above the Arctic Circle. Above this imaginary line, which circles the North Pole at a distance of 2,600 km (1,600 miles), the Sun does not rise on at least one day of the year.

After the snow melts in May or June, tundra plants have the chance to grow and bloom. Like all plants, they make their own food using sunlight, which most can do only during the 50- to 60-day summer growing season, when the temperature is usually above 3 °C (37 °F). Common plants here are mosses, sedges, and cotton grass.

Rocks and soil are coated by leaflike, hairy, or crusty lichen. Lichen is not a plant but a composite (made of different living things) of algae and fungi. Lichen and plants provide food for animals from musk oxen to bumblebees, which in turn are food for meat-eaters.

ARCTIC HARE

Up to 70 cm (28 in) long, the Arctic hare can bound at 60 km/h (40 miles per hour) on its long, strong back legs. In the southern tundra, its fur changes from white to brown in summer, but in the far north—where summers are even shorter—it stays white all year.

ARCTIC BUMBLEBEE

One of the few tundra bumblebees, this insect rests in the cone-shaped flowers of Arctic poppies, which reflect the Sun's heat onto its body. In each group of bees, known as a colony, only the queen survives the winter—by hibernating in a mammal burrow—then lays eggs in spring.

ARCTIC WOLF

Found only on the islands of Canada's far north, the Arctic wolf preys on musk oxen and Arctic hares. When summers are snowy, the number of these plant-eaters falls, soon followed by a drop in the number of wolves.

MUSK OX

Named for the musky smell given off by males to attract females, the musk ox has long, thick hair. It feeds on lichens, grasses, and mosses, digging with its hooves in the winter snow to find them.

TUNDRA STOAT

This mammal is in the mustelid family along with wolverines. It seizes small mammals, birds, and eggs with its sharp teeth. The tundra stoat has a brown summer coat, which gradually falls out before winter and grows back white and thicker.

CACKLING GOOSE

This bird nests on the summer tundra, but flies south for the winter. Eggs are laid near water, in a hollow made by the female and lined with plants and feathers. The goose eats water plants, which it reaches by tipping forward as it swims, dipping its head and neck.

Snowy Owl

The snowy owl is the largest bird of prey in the northernmost tundra. It has mostly white plumage, which keeps it camouflaged against snow. Like other birds of prey, it eats animals that are large compared with its own size, helped by a sharp, hooked beak and claws.

SKILLED HUNTER

The snowy owl watches for prey from a rock or mound. Like other owls, it can turn its head by 270 degrees, so it can see nearly all around and can pinpoint the direction of sounds by sensing when they are loudest in each ear. When the owl detects small animals—particularly rodents such as lemmings, mice, and voles— it swoops, thumping down hard on the animal with its strong claws, which are known as talons.

Small prey is often swallowed whole. Powerful stomach juices break down the flesh, while the indigestible bones, teeth, fur, and feathers are pressed into pellets that are brought back up 18 to 24 hours later.

TUNDRA TRAITS

A snowy owl can withstand temperatures as low as -62 °C (-80 °F) without appearing distressed. It has very dense feathers, with a thick layer of fluffy "down" feathers underneath its longer, stronger "flight" feathers. The feathers on its feet are longer than those of any other owl. During storms, the snowy owl is often seen sheltering behind rocks. Most owls hunt at night, but this owl must endure both the long winter night and the endless summer day, so it hunts for short periods during both night and day.

In the milder weather of May or early June, a female snowy owl lays around seven to nine eggs on higher ground on the tundra. For around a month, she sits on her eggs to warm them, while her male partner brings food. Newly hatched chicks are blind and rely on their parents for food. By late September, when the tundra is growing icier, the chicks can hunt on their own, just in time to fly southward to escape the winter. However, many adults, particularly older and larger birds, stay in the far north all year.

The fringed edges of the snowy owl's flight feathers help to dampen the sound of air passing over its wings as they beat, so the owl can hunt noiselessly.

Snowy Owl Facts

SPECIES	*Bubo scandiacus*
FAMILY	True owls
CLASS	Birds
SIZE	52–71 cm (20–28 in) long
RANGE	Far northern North America, Europe, and Asia
DIET	Small mammals and birds

Unlike its parents, a snowy owl chick has brown feathers, which keep it hidden among lichen and rocks.

Butterflies and Moths

As adults, these insects usually have four wings. Young butterflies and moths, known as caterpillars, are wingless before going through changes called metamorphosis. Butterflies and moths look similar, but butterflies have club-shaped tips on their antennae.

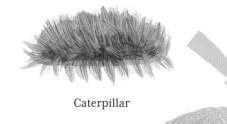

Caterpillar

Moth

Cocoon

ARCTIC WOOLLY BEAR MOTH

Most butterflies and moths spend a few weeks as a caterpillar, but this moth of the far north spends seven years as one, as a result of the long winters when it cannot eat or grow. As a caterpillar, it survives temperatures of -70 °C (-94 °F) by spending much of the year in a deep sleep, known as diapause, inside a silk cocoon it spins with another caterpillar. In the moth's final summer, it emerges from its cocoon as a winged adult.

ARCTIC BLUE

Arctic blue butterflies that live in the far north have darker wings than their southern relatives. Like most butterflies, the Arctic blue often rests with its wings open so that they can be warmed by sunlight. Darker wings soak up more heat than paler wings.

ARCTIC FRITILLARY

Female Arctic fritillaries live only long enough to mate and lay eggs on the leaves of dwarf willows and Arctic white heather, which the caterpillars will eat. As with all butterflies and moths, the caterpillars have strong jaws for chewing. Adults have only a tube-like mouthpart, called a proboscis, for sucking flower nectar.

PHOEBUS APOLLO

This butterfly has eye-like spots on its wings known as ocelli. These patterns may help the butterfly attract a mate, with butterflies that have bigger, brighter spots getting more mates. Ocelli may also frighten away predators, since the "eyes" seem to belong to a bigger animal.

Caterpillar

Butterfly

ISABELLA TIGER MOTH

Like most tundra moths and butterflies, this moth spends the winter as a caterpillar. After entering diapause, its heart stops beating and its body freezes solid. Yet the moth survives by making a chemical known as a cryoprotectant, which prevents its tissues from being damaged by freezing.

Caterpillar

Moth

NORTHERN CLOUDED YELLOW

Adult northern clouded yellows fly only during the brief summer months of June to August, when they suck nectar from the flowers of Arctic plants such as willows. As they feed, the butterflies carry pollen from flower to flower, enabling the plants to make new seeds.

Butterfly and Moth Facts

ORDER	Butterflies and moths
CLASS	Insects
SIZE	1.2–28 cm (0.5–11 in) wingspan
RANGE	All continents except Antarctica in all regions except polar ice
DIET	As adults, nectar, tree sap, and dung; as caterpillars, leaves and stems

Coniferous Forest

Female cone
releasing winged seeds

Female cone
growing seeds

Male cone

Female cone
ready for pollen

Coniferous trees have male and female cones.
Male cones make pollen, which is carried by the wind or
by insects to female cones, which can then make seeds.
When the seeds are ready, female cones open so that the
winged seeds can be spread by the wind.

Sandwiched between tundra to the north and deciduous forest to the south, most of the world's coniferous forests lie in a band across northern North America, Europe, and Asia. In Europe and Asia, these forests are often known as taiga, while in North America they may be called boreal forest. These regions are covered by coniferous trees, such as pines, spruces, and firs. Instead of making seeds in flowers, these trees make them in woody cones. Coniferous trees have needle-shaped or scale-shaped leaves. These tough, compact leaves are not damaged by cold, so can remain on the tree all year. Conifers are a type of "evergreen" tree because they stay green year-round.

The coniferous forest biome has long, cold winters with heavy snowfalls. The average winter temperature is around -20 °C (-4 °F). Yet at least 4 months of the year are without frost, giving plants a chance to grow. The average summer temperature is about 15 °C (59 °F). This biome also has enough rainfall, 30 to 90 cm (12 to 35 in) per year, to water trees. A few shrubs, grasses, and flowers grow beneath the trees in this region's poor soil.

Coniferous forests are home to more animals than polar and tundra regions, but far fewer than warmer forests. Most animals here rely on the trees for food or shelter—or hunt the animals that do. Animals can be found in each layer of the forest, from birds, spiders,

Siberian
chipmunk of
northern Asia

and climbing mammals in the branches, to earthworms and earwigs in the soil. Although the cold winters mean that there are few reptiles and amphibians, some hardy species can be found.

In the boreal forest of Alaska, in the United States, the black-capped chickadee stores seeds in summer so it has supplies for winter, when it often shelters in a tree hole. Another hole-user is the little brown bat, which rests in a tree in the daytime, but hunts for insects at night. In winter, it huddles with other bats to hibernate. Up to 2.1 m (6.9 ft) tall, the Alaska moose is active all year thanks to its thick skin and hair.

Siberian Taiga

Taiga covers 5.5 million sq km (2 million sq miles) of the Russian region of Siberia, where the temperature ranges from -65 °C (-85 °F) in winter to 40 °C (104 °F) in summer. Coniferous trees such as spruce, fir, larch, and pine grow as tall as 50 m (164 ft).

Most taiga animals have a thick layer of fur or feathers, which is insulation (preventing heat from passing through) to keep them warm in winter but cool in summer. Small animals also find protection from the winter cold in their environment, by sheltering in a tree hole or beneath the snow.

The majority of taiga birds avoid the winter by flying south, but many mammals hibernate in a warm den, sleeping so deeply they have little or no need for food. Many insects—and the few amphibians and reptiles—hibernate so deeply their body freezes, then thaws in spring.

EURASIAN LYNX

Up to 1.3 m (4.3 ft) long, this wild cat has large, furry paws, with webbing (flaps of skin) between the toes, which spread its weight on snow so it does not sink in. The lynx hunts for rabbits, rodents, foxes, and deer.

SIBERIAN SALAMANDER

This amphibian freezes solid during its winter hibernation. Hidden among moss, the salamander's heart stops beating, but its tissues are not damaged due to special chemicals in its blood.

SPOTTED NUTCRACKER

This bird uses its large, pointed beak to rip open pine cones to get the seeds inside. Then it holds the seeds with its forked, hardened tongue as it cracks them open with its beak.

SIBERIAN MUSK DEER

Unlike most male deer, which grow antlers on their head to attract females, the male musk deer grows extra-long teeth called tusks. The male also makes a strong-smelling liquid that he wipes on branches to mark his territory.

SIBERIAN TIGER

Well camouflaged among tree trunks by its stripes, the Siberian tiger stalks its prey—including deer, wild boar, and elk—until close enough to pounce. Then it grasps the animal's neck with its powerful jaws and sharp teeth, which grow to 7.5 cm (3 in) long.

COMMON LIZARD

Found farther north than any other reptile, this lizard does not lay eggs like most reptiles. It gives birth to live young, which are better able to survive the cold than eggs. The lizard hibernates under a log in winter and often lies in a sunny spot in summer.

Northwestern Wolf

This North American wolf can run swiftly through snow on its long legs. In winter, its coat is thick and fluffy, but it sheds some hair in summer. In freezing temperatures, it rests by placing its nose between its back legs and covering its face with its bushy tail.

A FAMILY DOG

Weighing up to 72 kg (159 lb), the northwestern wolf is the largest subspecies of wolf, which is the largest species in the dog family. The family includes foxes, coyotes, jackals, and pet dogs, which are descended from wild wolves that were first captured and tamed by humans around 15,000 years ago.

The wolf is a social animal, which means it usually lives in a group, known as a pack. A northwestern wolf pack has around eight members: usually a male–female pair and their children. Pack members communicate with each other using howls, growls, and whines. They also use body language to show friendliness or aggression. Face-licking and cheek-rubbing show friendliness, while an older male wolf may bare his teeth, stand tall, and raise the hair on his neck to dominate other wolves.

Northwestern Wolf Facts

SUBSPECIES	*Canis lupus occidentalis*
FAMILY	Dogs
CLASS	Mammals
SIZE	1.6–2.1 m (5.2–7 ft) long
RANGE	Northwestern North America from Alaska to Wyoming
DIET	Moose, bison, elk, caribou, snowshoe hares, voles, lemmings, and ground squirrels

NIGHT HUNTER

The northwestern wolf usually hunts at night. It can travel up to 95 km (60 miles) in one night as it tracks prey using its powerful sense of smell. In winter, when prey is scarce, the wolf usually hunts in a pack, which brings more success with large prey, such as moose. In summer, adult wolves may hunt alone, often by lying in wait for smaller prey.

Small prey, such as rodents, can be killed instantly with a bite from a wolf's sharp, strong front teeth, which grow 6 cm (2.4 in) long. When hunting large, hard-hoofed prey, a wolf risks serious injury. If it manages to inflict a bite, a wolf may withdraw to safety, waiting for the animal to weaken before it goes in for the kill.

Without hurting each other, wolf pups often play at fighting. This helps them learn the skills they will need as adults for hunting and defending themselves.

Northwestern wolves can reach
64 km/h (40 miles per hour) as
they chase fast-moving prey,
such as the snowshoe hare.
This hare is named for its wide
back feet, which prevent it
from sinking into snow.

Rodents

Coniferous forests are home to many tree-dwelling rodents with short,
sharp claws for climbing trees. These mammals have long, sharp front teeth that
grow continuously, but are worn down by gnawing food and burrowing.
Out of around 4,000 species of mammals, 1,500 are rodents.

NORTHERN FLYING SQUIRREL

This rodent can glide from higher to
lower branches due to a thick fold of skin,
called a patagium, which runs from each
front leg to back leg. When gliding, the
flying squirrel spreads its limbs wide,
forming a parachute. Its longest glides
are more than 45 m (148 ft).

RED SQUIRREL

The red squirrel uses its long tail for balance as it jumps
from branch to branch. In parts of Great Britain, Ireland, and
Italy, this squirrel has been driven out by the eastern gray
squirrel, which was brought from North America by humans.
Gray squirrels are larger and carry diseases that kill red
squirrels but not themselves.

NORTH AMERICAN PORCUPINE

A porcupine has 30,000 quills growing
from its skin, apart from on its face,
belly, and feet. Quills are thick, hard
hairs that are formed into sharp
spines. When threatened, a porcupine
raises its quills, so that they stick into
an attacker's skin—and stay stuck long
after detaching from the porcupine.

NORTHERN RED-BACKED VOLE

Like many other rodents, this vole is camouflaged among trees, rocks, and soil by its dappled brown fur. It nests in a short burrow or beneath a rock. In winter, it stays active by building tunnels beneath the snow, which give protection from cold and predators such as foxes.

EASTERN DEER MOUSE

This deer mouse makes a nest of grass and moss in tall, hollow trees of North American forests. During the safety of night, it emerges to hunt for seeds, leaves, spiders, and caterpillars. During the winter cold, the deer mouse shares a nest with up to ten others.

SIBERIAN CHIPMUNK

In winter, this chipmunk stays in its underground burrow, where it has stored 3–4 kg (6.6–8.8 lb) of seeds. This food is transported in pouches in the chipmunk's cheeks, which can reach the size of the chipmunk's body when full. The burrow, up to 2.5 m (8.2 ft) long and with separate storage and waste areas, is often shared with another chipmunk.

Rodent Facts

ORDER	Rodents
CLASS	Mammals
SIZE	12–134 cm (5–53 in) long
RANGE	All continents except Antarctica but also absent from some islands
DIET	Seeds, stems, leaves, nuts, insects, worms, and other small animals

Mountains

Snow zone

Alpine zone

Montane zone

Lowland zone

The conditions on a mountain are different from in the valleys below. As we climb a mountain and our height above sea level grows, the air becomes thinner, as gravity—the force that pulls air toward the ground—is weaker farther from Earth's core. Thinner air is colder and drier, so the temperature falls and there is less rain. In addition, it is often windy on mountains because they are exposed, with no obstacles to slow the wind.

Different communities of plants live at different heights on mountains. The lower slopes of mountains are often forested, in a region known as the montane zone. The montane zone ends at the tree line, above which it is too cold for trees to grow. The height of a mountain's tree line depends on its distance from the equator, but it ranges from around 3,500 m (11,500 ft) near the equator to 500 m (1,640 ft) in northern Europe. Above the tree line is the alpine zone, where plants are small and low, hugging the ground to survive the cold and wind. Higher still on a mountain's slopes is the snow line, above which the ground is covered by snow. Very few plants survive above the snow line, with the highest plant of all a moss that lives at 6,480 m (21,260 ft) on Mount Everest, the world's tallest mountain.

Mountain animals must survive the cold and wind. Many are insulated with thick layers of fur or feathers.

Coniferous trees often grow in the montane zone, where they are able to withstand the cold, windy conditions. Above the tree line, in the alpine zone, shrubs and grasses give way to mosses, lichens, and bare rock. Higher still, a peak may be crowned by snow and ice.

Markhor of Asia's
Karakoram and
Himalaya Mountains

They also have shorter legs, tails, and ears so they lose less heat from their body surface. During the winter, many hibernate or migrate to warmer regions. To survive the thin air, which offers less oxygen than the air below, mountain animals may have larger lungs to take in as much oxygen as possible.

In Asia's Himalaya Mountains, the snow leopard has small ears; wide paws so that it does not sink into snow; and a long, flexible tail that helps it balance as it leaps. Up to 2 m (6.6 ft) tall, the wild yak is one of the few mammals the big cat cannot kill. Perching on a crag up to 5,500 m (18,000 ft) above sea level, the Himalayan vulture watches the leopard closely, hoping to feed on the remains of its kills.

Andes Mountains

The Andes Mountains stretch for 7,000 km (4,350 miles) through western South America. In the central Andes is the Altiplano (meaning "high plain"), a vast region of flat, mostly treeless land with an average height of 3,750 m (12,300 ft).

Most plants on the Altiplano are grasses and low shrubs, so animals find little shelter from heat or cold. They face extremes of temperature: Summer days reach 24 °C (75 °F), but winter nights fall to -20 °C (-4 °F). Many animals stay comfortable by swapping between basking in the sunshine and sheltering in a burrow or beneath rocks.

Altiplano mammals have evolved to survive the thin air, often by having very efficient hearts and extra blood cells for carrying oxygen around their body. Birds are among the most common animals here, because their lungs can extract more oxygen from air than those of mammals.

DARWIN'S RHEA

A relative of ostriches and emus, the rhea is a flightless bird with weak wings. Up to 1 m (3.3 ft) tall, it uses its long legs to run from predators, such as Andean mountain cats, at 60 km/h (37 miles per hour).

MONTANE GUINEA PIG

This wild guinea pig is an ancestor of pet guinea pigs. It shelters from the weather and predators by trampling runways through grasses, so it stays hidden as it searches for leaves and fruit to eat.

ANDEAN CONDOR

The world's largest bird of prey, the Andean condor weighs up to 15 kg (33 lb) and has a wingspan (from wingtip to wingtip) of up to 3.3 m (10.8 ft). The condor lays its eggs on rocky ledges as high as 5,000 m (16,000 ft), where predators cannot reach.

VICUÑA

The vicuña has very thick, soft wool, which keeps it warm at heights of up to 4,800 m (15,700 ft). During the day, it eats grass on the alpine plain, but it climbs rocky slopes at night for safety. It is a camelid, making it a relative of camels and llamas.

ANDEAN HAIRY ARMADILLO

This mammal is protected from attack by 18 bony plates on its back. It shelters in a burrow dug with its paws, emerging to find seeds and insects using its long nose. In summer, it is nocturnal to stay cool, but in winter it is active during the day to keep warm.

LIOLAEMUS MULTIFORMIS LIZARD

This lizard can warm itself 25 °C (45 °F) above the air temperature by sunbathing for most of the day. Its brown skin can soak up more heat than paler skin. It shelters in a burrow at night.

Red Panda

The red panda lives in forests between 2,000 and 4,300 m (6,600 and 14,100 ft) above sea level, in the montane zone of the Himalayas. It feeds mainly on the leaves of bamboo, a type of grass with a tall, thick, hollow stem.

TWO PANDAS

The red panda shares its preferred food, bamboo, with the giant panda. Both mammals have an extended wrist bone forming a thumb-like structure that helps them grasp bamboo stems. The word "panda" may come from the Nepali word *paũjā*, which means paw. Despite their similarities, the two animals are not close relatives. The giant panda is a bear, while the red panda is more closely related to mustelids such as raccoons and weasels.

In parts of China, the red and the giant panda live in the same areas. However, they do not compete with each other for the same bamboo. Larger than its namesake at up to 1.9 m (6.2 ft) long, the giant panda stays on gentle mountain slopes with more widely spaced bamboo stems. The red panda prefers steep slopes with close-growing bamboo, where it can more easily hide or climb away from predators such as snow leopards.

TREE CLIMBER

The red panda usually eats during twilight and night. In the daytime, it sleeps in the safety of tree branches. On summer days, it stays cool by dangling its legs in the air. In winter, when the temperature can drop below freezing, it curls into a ball with its bushy tail over its face. Its strong, curved claws can grasp the tree trunk as it climbs and descends, which it does head first with its back legs squeezing the trunk.

The red, white, and black fur of the red panda helps it stay camouflaged. Among the dappled shade of tree trunks and bamboo stems, the red panda's pattern breaks up its outline, making it harder to spot. The red fur blends in well among trees covered with red moss or lichen. The panda's fur contains long, waterproof hairs as well as a thick, fluffy, warm undercoat.

Red Panda Facts

SPECIES	*Ailurus fulgens*
FAMILY	Ailurids
CLASS	Mammals
SIZE	79–112 cm (31–44 in) long
RANGE	Eastern Himalaya Mountains of Asia
DIET	Bamboo leaves and shoots, fruits, bird eggs, insects, and lizards

The giant panda's white and black fur is camouflage among snowy slopes and bamboo stems. Like the red panda, it is threatened by the loss of its forest habitat.

A red panda spends around 12 hours a day sleeping or resting. An adult red panda usually lives alone, except during the mating season.

Goat-Antelopes

These plant-eating mammals have hooves split into two toes. Most males and many females have horns. Hooves and horns are covered in keratin, a hard material also found in human nails and hair. Wild goat-antelopes live in the mountains or other extreme habitats, such as tundra, where there are fewer predators.

TAKIN

This large Asian goat-antelope weighs up to 350 kg (770 lb). Female and young takins live in herds, but adult males usually live alone except in the mating season. When bears or wolves approach, takins give a cough-like alarm call, then hides in thickets of bamboo.

MOUFLON

Farmed sheep are descended from mouflons first domesticated in western Asia around 10,000 years ago. Male mouflons fight each other over females, but afterward the males graze side by side, with the loser licking the winner's neck as a show of friendliness.

HIMALAYAN TAHR

The tahr has backward-curving horns to prevent injuries during headbutting contests between males. During the mating season, males compete for the right to mate with the most females. Tahrs have rubbery hooves, which help them grip smooth rocks.

CHAMOIS

In the mountains of Europe and western Asia, the chamois feeds on grass and flowers above the tree line in summer. In winter, it descends to coniferous forests, where it eats bark and needle leaves. It escapes from predators by leaping from rock to rock, jumping 2 m (6.6 ft) up into the air or across a gap of 6 m (20 ft).

TIBETAN ANTELOPE

The Tibetan antelope lives at heights of 3,250 to 5,500 m (10,660 to 18,040 ft) on the Tibetan Plateau, a vast area of high, flat land in Asia. To stay warm, it has a thick layer of soft underfur. To cope with the low level of oxygen in the thin air, the cells in its blood are particularly effective at delivering oxygen around its body.

MARKHOR

This goat is related to the goats kept on farms, which are descended from wild goats first captured around 10,000 years ago. The markhor lives in the Himalayan and Karakoram Mountains in Asia. Its coat is short during the warm summer, but grows long and thick in winter.

Goat-Antelope Facts

SUBFAMILY	Goat-antelopes
CLASS	Mammals
SIZE	1–2.5 m (3.3–8.2 ft) long
RANGE	Mountain, tundra, and desert in North America, Europe, Africa, and Asia
DIET	Grasses, shrubs, twigs, fruits, nuts, and mosses

Temperate Forest

Sunlight

Oxygen

Carbon dioxide

Sugar

Water

Plants are usually green because they contain a green chemical called chlorophyll. This chemical soaks up sunlight, which the plant uses as energy to make sugar and oxygen from water and carbon dioxide, a gas found in the air. The sugar is used as food, while the oxygen is released into the air. The leaves of deciduous trees often turn yellow or red before they fall as they lose their chlorophyll.

Temperate forest and woodland is in the world's temperate zone, between the polar and tropical zones. The temperate zone forms two bands running from around 2,600 to 7,500 km (1,615 to 4,660 miles) both north and south of the equator. This region usually has warm summers and cool winters. The types of trees found in a temperate forest or woodland depend on the particular area's rainfall and temperature. In a woodland, trees are more widely spaced than in a forest.

Deciduous forests are found mainly in the temperate zone of North America, Europe, and eastern Asia. These regions have moderate rainfall and winter temperatures that may dip below freezing. Deciduous trees (deciduous means "falling off") lose their leaves before winter. They are "broadleaf" trees with wide, flat leaves that are damaged by cold, so they are dropped to save energy. Deciduous broadleaf trees include maple, beech, and chestnut. In warmer regions of the temperate zone, such as southern Europe and southern Australia, forests of evergreen broadleaf trees are found. These trees, such as olive, cork oak, and eucalyptus, never drop all their leaves at once.

A wide range of invertebrates, amphibians, reptiles, birds, and mammals live in temperate forests and woodlands. Many feed on tree parts and products—

Acorn woodpecker of southwestern North America

including leaves, flowers, fruits, nuts, bark, and sap— while avoiding predators from bears to spiders. In deciduous forests, animals must survive the cool winter and the loss of shelter as trees drop their leaves. In warm, dry evergreen forests, animals must escape the wildfires that may rage in summer.

In Poland and Belarus, Białowieża Forest is a mixed temperate forest of deciduous and coniferous trees. The forest's largest inhabitant is the European bison, Europe's heaviest mammal at up to 1,000 kg (2,200 lb). Nearby, a wild boar searches for roots, nuts, mushrooms, and invertebrates. It fails to notice a procession of European red wood ants, which have built a nest mound 1.4 m (4.5 ft) high from twigs and pine needles.

Australian Eucalyptus Forest

Eucalyptus forest covers around 1 million sq km (385,000 sq miles) of Australia. There are over 700 species of eucalyptus trees and shrubs, most of them evergreen, with names such as river red gum, stringybark, and silvertop ash.

Eucalyptus forests are often in areas with long, dry summers where wildfires are common. Yet many eucalyptus trees resprout quickly after a fire. Others have seeds that are cracked open by the heat of fire and start to grow in the sunlit space cleared by the blaze.

Animals of the eucalyptus forests can sense fires before humans do. They flee by flying, hopping, or running to gullies or rivers, climbing higher, or hiding in burrows. However, global warming is resulting in more wildfires, putting these forests and their animals at risk.

LACE MONITOR

Up to 2 m (6.6 ft) long, this lizard searches the ground for insects, reptiles, small mammals, and any animal that is already dead. Using its long, sharp claws, it also climbs trees to reach birds' nests, where it takes both eggs and chicks.

COMMON WOMBAT

This plant-eater digs an extensive tunnel system, with branching tunnels up to 20 m (65 ft) long and many side entrances. It hides in its tunnels during the daytime. During wildfires, the tunnels are also used by animals including wallabies, snakes, possums, and bandicoots.

KOALA

The koala has few competitors for food since it eats only eucalyptus leaves, which are poisonous to many animals. These leaves offer little energy, so the koala spends up to 22 hours a day sleeping in the safety of a tree.

RED-TAILED BLACK COCKATOO

This parrot feeds on the seeds of eucalyptus trees such as desert and brown stringybark. It can hold a seed or branch with one clawed foot, usually the left one, while standing on the other foot.

RAINBOW LORIKEET

This bird feeds on nectar and pollen from eucalyptus flowers, using its long, bristle-tipped tongue to reach inside and lap them up. The lorikeet's bright plumage helps it to be recognized by others of its species.

RED-NECKED WALLABY

A wallaby travels by hopping, using its long back legs and strong tail. Like the koala and wombat, it is a marsupial mammal. Found mostly in Australia and South America, marsupials give birth to tiny, undeveloped babies, which they carry in a pouch on their abdomen.

Red Deer

These hoofed plant-eaters live in temperate forest, woodland, grassland, and moorland. Male red deer, known as stags, grow antlers ready for each mating season, then shed them afterward. Antlers are extensions of the skull, made from hard bone and bendier cartilage, covered by skin.

THE RUT

Adult male and female red deer live separately for most of the year, but they come together for the mating season, known as the rut. During the rut, stags compete for the attention of females. First, the stags walk side by side, making loud roars as they examine the size of each other's antlers and body. At this stage, smaller or younger stags back down.

When two stags refuse to back down, they clash with their antlers, sometimes hurting each other. The winners of these fights are followed by a group of up to 20 females, known as a harem. The losing males also lose the chance to mate for that year.

FOUR STOMACHS

The red deer belongs to a group of animals called ruminants (from the Latin for "to chew again"), which includes deer, goats, antelopes, and cattle. These animals have a four-chambered stomach that breaks down tough plant material by fermenting it. Fermentation is when tiny living things such as bacteria—which live in the first chamber of the deer's stomach—release chemicals that break down plants.

After fermented food has passed through the first stomach chamber, it moves into the second chamber. Here food separates into liquid and solid material, called cud, which the deer brings back up into its mouth and rechews, before swallowing it again. After food is further broken down in the last two stomach chambers, nutrients are soaked up by the walls of the deer's intestines, and waste is expelled as poop.

After a red deer has filled its first stomach, it sits down to chew cud in a well-hidden spot. A female deer (pictured) is known as a hind.

Fights between stags ensure that only the strongest, healthiest males get the chance to mate. This increases the chance that young deer, known as fawns, will also be healthy.

Red Deer Facts

SPECIES	*Cervus elaphus*
FAMILY	Deer
CLASS	Mammals
SIZE	1.7–2.7 m (5.6–8.9 ft) long
RANGE	Europe, southwestern Asia, and northern Africa
DIET	Grasses, tree shoots, sedges, and shrubs

Woodpeckers

Woodpeckers use their strong beak to drill into tree trunks to find small animals that live in wood. They also use their beak to dig nest holes in trees. A woodpecker's zygodactyl feet— with two toes pointing forward and two backward—are suited to holding on to trunks.

NORTHERN FLICKER

To keep other woodpeckers out of its territory, the northern flicker drums with its beak on trees or even metal roofs, poles, and pipes, making a loud and startling noise. It catches ants by drilling into their nests, then rubs them over its feathers to spread their formic acid, which kills tiny insects and mites that irritate the woodpecker's skin.

ACORN WOODPECKER

This woodpecker lives in oak woodlands and forests, where it feeds on the fruits of the oak tree, known as acorns. It stores collected acorns by drilling acorn-sized holes in tree trunks then placing them inside. As each acorn dries and shrinks, it is moved to a smaller hole.

EUROPEAN GREEN WOODPECKER

Despite the red feathers on its head, the green woodpecker is well camouflaged among leaves. It is rarely seen but can often be heard making its "kyu-kyu-kyuck" call to warn other woodpeckers away from its territory. Like all woodpeckers, it has a long, sticky tongue, which it uses for catching ants.

PILEATED WOODPECKER

Like other woodpeckers, the pileated woodpecker has a straight, sharp beak suited to drilling wood and a stiff tail for supporting itself on trunks as it works. During the mating season, this woodpecker often uses its beak to drum loudly on hollow trunks to attract a mate.

RED-BELLIED WOODPECKER

A pair of male and female red-bellied woodpeckers drill a nest together in a dead or dying tree. Some pairs return to each other for several mating seasons and use the same tree year after year. The nest is used for resting and sleeping as well as for laying eggs.

GREAT SPOTTED WOODPECKER

Like most woodpeckers, this woodpecker lays eggs in a hole drilled in a tree trunk. The great spotted woodpecker lays four to six white eggs. Both parents sit on the eggs to warm them, then share the work of cleaning the nest and feeding the chicks after they hatch.

Woodpecker Facts

FAMILY	Woodpeckers
CLASS	Birds
SIZE	7–58 cm (3–23 in) long
RANGE	North America, South America, Europe, Africa, and Asia
DIET	Insects, spiders, nuts, fruits, and tree sap

Grassland

Found in temperate and tropical regions, grassland is a wide area where the most common plants are grasses. Grassland is given different names around the world: prairie in central North America, pampas in southern South America, steppe in central Asia, and savanna in south-central Africa. Grassland may be dotted with shrubs or trees, but most trees cannot grow because of low rainfall, frequent wildfires, and constant nibbling by plant-eaters. However, the rainfall in a grassland region is enough to nourish grasses, which also grow back quickly after fire, dry weather, or a cold winter.

Grasslands receive around 50 to 90 cm (20 to 35 in) of rain per year. Taller grasses grow in areas of higher rainfall, with North America's prairie having longer grasses than Asia's steppe. Grasses range from around 2 m (6.6 ft) to 20 cm (8 in) tall. Temperate grasslands usually have hot summers and cold winters, with a temperature range as wide as -40 °C (-40 °F) in winter and 38 °C (100 °F) in summer. Tropical grasslands are hot all year, but have a distinct dry season and wet season, when most of the year's rain falls. Temperate grassland has rich soil, which has led to much of it being turned over to farming, particularly in North America.

Grasslands are home to many grazing mammals, such as zebras, which feed on grasses and other low plants.

Around half of North America's grassland has been turned over to farming. The most important crop is wheat, a grass grown for its seeds, which are cereal grains. Many grassland birds, such as red-winged blackbirds, have adapted to living on farmland.

Giant carrion beetle of North American grasslands

Where trees and shrubs are found, there are also browsing mammals, such as giraffes, which eat higher-growing plants. Since there is plentiful food and space for plant-eaters, some—such as bison and elephants—grow very large. Large plant-eaters are food for large meat-eaters, including lions and coyotes. Smaller animals—from mice to snakes—burrow or hide among the grasses to shelter from predators.

On the North American prairie, a male greater prairie chicken tries to attract a female by inflating air sacs on his neck and snapping his tail. Beneath his feet is a colony of hundreds of black-tailed prairie dogs. The colony digs a burrow system where these rodents can shelter from heat, cold, and predators such as the coyote. A member of the dog family, the sharp-toothed coyote grows up to 1.5 m (4.9 ft) long.

African Savanna

The plains of the African savanna are covered by tall grasses but also dotted with trees such as umbrella acacias and bush willows. These hardy plants can survive the long dry seasons, which are followed by rainy seasons that bring much-needed water.

The African savanna is home to large herds of mammals that graze on grass or browse on trees and shrubs. These herds are preyed on by predators including big cats, hyenas, and wild dogs, with scavengers feeding on leftovers.

Every dry season, herds of zebras and wildebeest walk many hundreds of miles in search of water and fresh grass. This season also sees wildfires sweep across the parched plains. Many animals flee or burrow to safety. They return once the trees and grasses grow new shoots.

AFRICAN BUSH ELEPHANT

Weighing up to 10,400 kg (22,900 lb), this elephant is the world's largest land animal. During the wet season, it feeds on grasses. In the dry season, when the grasses die back, it rips off tree bark with its strong tusks and uses its muscly trunk to dig in the soil for water.

GIRAFFE

This browser is the world's tallest land animal, growing up to 5.7 m (18.7 ft) tall. Its long neck and legs allow it to reach into trees to feed on leaves, fruit, and flowers, escaping competition with shorter plant-eaters. Like humans, giraffes have seven neck bones—called cervical vertebrae—but each one is over 28 cm (11 in) long.

LEOPARD

The leopard grows up to 3 m (9.8 ft) long, including its muscly tail, which is used for balance while chasing prey and climbing trees. This big cat hunts at nighttime, then spends the day sleeping in a tree.

LAPPET-FACED VULTURE

This vulture is a scavenger, flying over the savanna in search of animals that have been killed by predators or disease. Its featherless head is easy to clean after reaching into a carcass.

PLAINS ZEBRA

A member of the horse family, the plains zebra lives in herds of up to 1,000 animals. Each zebra has a different pattern of dark and light stripes. The pattern protects the zebra from biting flies, which find it harder to make out the zebra's outline.

SPOTTED HYENA

The spotted hyena is the most common predator on the African savanna due to its ability to change its strategy whenever needed. It is able to hunt alone or in a group and will scavenge when live prey is scarce.

Lion

This big cat once roamed across Africa, southern Europe, and southwestern Asia. Today, humans have driven lions from everywhere except savanna and shrubland in Africa and western India. Most lions live in family groups called prides, but young adults may spend years hunting alone before joining a pride.

LIFE IN A PRIDE

Male lions are larger than females, which are called lionesses. When males are around a year old, they start to grow longer hair on their head, shoulders, and chest, called a mane. Healthier, older males have darker and thicker manes. A thick mane may protect the neck from teeth and claws during fights with other males, but it is probably most useful for attracting females. When choosing a mate, lionesses prefer lions with thick manes.

Lions spend around 20 hours a day sleeping or resting, often in the shade of a tree. When the temperature falls at dusk, lions wake and begin to play or groom each other with their tongues.

On the African savanna, lions often hunt blue wildebeest. Lions can open their jaws to up 28 cm (11 in) wide, then stab with sharp canines 7 cm (3 in) long.

SKILLED HUNTERS

Most hunting is done around dusk and dawn, when the temperature is lower than in the heat of day. Lions stalk prey by closing in slowly and silently, relying on their golden fur and the dim light for camouflage among the dry grass.

When lions are close to their prey, they make a sudden rush and leap, killing with a bite to the throat. Male lions hunt alone, but much of a pride's hunting is done by groups of lionesses. Each lioness plays a particular role in hunts, such as stalking prey on the left or right. Usually, food is shared with the rest of the pride.

A lioness gives birth to up to four cubs in a den among rocks or shrubs. For the first six months, she feeds the cubs on her milk.

Lion Facts

SPECIES	*Panthera leo*
FAMILY	Cats
CLASS	Mammals
SIZE	2.3–3 m (7.5–9.8 ft) long
RANGE	Africa south of the Sahara Desert, and western India
DIET	Mammals including blue wildebeest, plains zebras, giraffes, and deer

Beetles

These insects have two pairs of wings: a flexible interior pair used for flight and a tough exterior pair for protection. There are around 400,000 species of beetles, making up a quarter of all animal species. On grasslands, many beetles play the vital role of helping to spread seeds and break down waste.

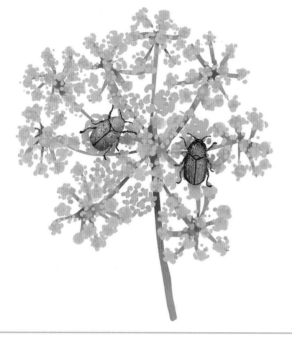

SILKY HIDDEN-HEAD LEAF BEETLE

This beetle feeds on wildflower pollen, particularly from yellow umbellifer flowers. Males are golden-green, and females are bronze. Their shining exoskeletons, which glint different shades from different angles, are believed to attract a mate and distract predators.

MINOTAUR BEETLE

After mating, this European dung beetle digs a tunnel up to 1.5 m (4.9 ft) deep, where it stores the dung (poop) of rabbits and other plant-eaters. The female lays eggs by the dung, which is eaten by the young larvae after hatching. By burying plant-eater dung, this beetle spreads seeds and returns plant nutrients to the soil, which helps new plants grow.

OHLONE TIGER BEETLE

Found only in the coastal grasslands of Santa Cruz County, California, in the United States, this beetle hunts for small prey in the patches of bare soil between tufts of grass. Its long legs help it run fast, while its large jaws—known as mandibles—grab wriggling prey.

PIE-DISH BEETLE

Found in the dry grasslands and shrublands of Australia, this beetle is named for its flattened body shape and the broad rims on its body and outer wings. These rims protect the beetle's head, legs, and underside from attack by predators such as spiders.

GIANT CARRION BEETLE

This North American beetle feeds on carrion (dead animals). A male and female carrion beetle bury a dead animal, such as a bird or rodent, then the female lays eggs beside the body, so that her larvae will have food after hatching. Adult carrion beetles bury themselves in soil to survive the winter cold.

ZAMBESI SCARAB BEETLE

This nocturnal dung beetle uses its sense of smell to find antelope dung, then rolls the dung quickly away, digs a burrow, and feasts on it. The beetle can roll its dung in a perfectly straight line across the savanna by navigating using patterns in moonlight that are invisible to human eyes.

Beetle Facts

ORDER	Beetles
CLASS	Insects
SIZE	0.03–13.5 cm (0.01–5.3 in) long
RANGE	Most land and freshwater habitats in the Americas, Europe, Africa, Asia, and Australasia
DIET	Plants, dung, carrion, and small invertebrates

Shrubland

Immortelle

French lavender

Corsican heath butterfly

Rosemary

On the French island of Corsica, shrubs of the maquis include immortelle, sometimes known as the curry plant because of the strong smell of its leaves; French lavender, which is used to prepare perfumes; and rosemary, which has fragrant, needle-like leaves used in cooking.

Shrubland, also known as scrubland or bush, is an area where most plants are evergreen shrubs, which grow alongside grasses and other small flowering plants. Shrubs have hard, woody stems. Unlike trees, which have a single woody stem, shrubs have several stems and grow less than 8 m (26 ft) tall. In some regions, shrubland has a specific name, such as maquis in southern France, fynbos in South Africa, and chaparral in the United States.

Many shrublands are in coastal regions with a Mediterranean climate: a dry, hot summer and a mild, wet winter. These conditions are found in southern Europe around the Mediterranean Sea, as well as other warm regions, including the southwestern United States, southern Africa, and southern Australia. Shrubland receives more rain than desert but less than most forests: between 20 and 100 cm (8 and 39 in) per year. In coastal regions, shrubland's tough, small-leafed shrubs have adapted to survive ocean winds, salty air and soil, and summer droughts. In addition, wildfires are common in summer, often caused by lightning. Wildfires prevent the growth of most trees, yet shrubland plants have evolved to survive them, often by regrowing quickly from their below-soil stem.

Shrubland animals must survive wildfires, drying winds, and lack of water in summer. Yet the thick vegetation is

Cyprus warbler of the eastern Mediterranean

shelter for insects, nesting birds, and small mammals. Due to their need for water, few amphibians live in shrubland, but some survive by burrowing into the soil during summer. Reptiles adjust their activity to the weather, moving between sunny and shady areas to maintain their temperature.

In Italy's coastal shrubland, a Hermann's tortoise crops plants using its hard, horny beak. In winter, this reptile hibernates under a shrub, where it also shelters from the summer midday Sun. Nearby lurks a conehead mantis (below left), which is well camouflaged by its green and pink legs and body, which resemble a budding twig. It is watching a Raymond's bush-cricket—which it will seize with its front legs. Both insects will die before winter, after laying their eggs.

Californian Chaparral

Shrubland known as chaparral covers around 121,000 sq km (47,000 sq miles) of California and Oregon, in the United States, and northern Mexico. The word "chaparral" comes from the Spanish for scrub oak, a small shrubby oak that reaches 1 to 2 m (3.3 to 6.6 ft) tall.

Despite cities and farms, wide stretches of California's coastal hills are chaparral. The summer here is very dry, with temperatures often higher than 37 °C (99 °F). Today, global warming is causing even drier summers, which lead to more wildfires, putting this habitat at risk.

Most chaparral plants, such as yuccas and creosote bushes, have hard leaves that can protect the water taken from their wide, deep roots. Chaparral animals have evolved to survive on little water, with many getting much of their water from eating plants.

GREATER ROADRUNNER

A member of the cuckoo order of birds, the strong-footed roadrunner walks more than it flies, reaching a speed of 32 km/h (20 miles per hour) as it runs after prey. It often eats lizards, venomous snakes, and tarantulas.

BLAINVILLE'S HORNED LIZARD

This lizard's wide, spiked body makes it harder for predators to swallow. In addition, it frightens predators away by pumping blood into the tissues around its eyes until they burst— spraying blood up to 1.2 m (4 ft).

COSTA'S HUMMINGBIRD

A male Costa's hummingbird has shining purple feathers on its throat, which attract a female. It uses its long, thin beak to reach into desert lavender and fairy duster flowers to drink nectar, as it hovers by beating its wings around 50 times per second.

CALIFORNIA YUCCA MOTH

A female yucca moth collects pollen from one chaparral yucca flower and carries it to another, where she lays an egg. The pollinated flower now makes lots of seeds—and the moth's larva feeds on some. Both plant and insect benefit from this symbiotic (meaning "living together") relationship.

CALIFORNIA EBONY TARANTULA

California's largest spider, this tarantula grows up to 13 cm (5 in) across and can live for 25 years. Like most tarantulas, its body is covered in bristly hairs that brush off on attackers, irritating their skin and eyes.

DESERT WOODRAT

This small rodent eats plants such as creosote bushes and sagebrush. For protection from predators, it builds a house from sticks and stems. As much as 1 m (3.3 ft) around at its base, the house has up to eight chambers for storing food and sleeping.

Cape Honeybee

**This honeybee lives in the fynbos shrubland of South Africa's Western Cape.
It plays a crucial role by pollinating many of the region's flowering plants. The fynbos
is home to nearly 6,000 species of plants that are found nowhere else on Earth.**

BUSY BEE

Like other honeybees, the Cape honeybee feeds on the
pollen and nectar of flowering plants. As it feeds, pollen
collects on its hair and is carried from one flower to
another—allowing the plants to reproduce. The Cape
honeybee lives in a hive with up to 80,000 other bees,
known as a colony. Most bees in a colony are female
worker bees, while a few hundred are male drone bees.
Each colony has a larger queen bee.

Collector worker bees use a straw-like mouthpart,
known as a proboscis, to suck nectar from flowers. After
returning to the hive, the collectors give the nectar to
house worker bees, which turn it into honey by drying it.
As collector bees visit flowers, their hairy legs get covered
with pollen, which collects in dips on their back legs
known as pollen baskets. Worker bees eat as much pollen
and nectar as they need, then store the rest in the hive.

LIFE IN A HIVE

Usually found in a hollow tree trunk, a honeybee hive
is constructed from beeswax, which is made by glands
on a worker bee's abdomen. The hive contains many
hexagonal cells, in which the queen lays eggs. These
hatch into wingless, legless larvae, which are fed a mix
of pollen and nectar, called beebread, by nurse worker
bees. After a week, the nurse bees close the cells, and
the larvae pupate, a life stage when they change into
adult bees.

Male drone bees live only long enough to mate with the
queen. Worker bees live for a few months, while the
queen may live for 3 or 4 years. When the queen grows
old, nurse worker bees create a new queen by feeding
some female larvae lots of a rich food made in glands
on their head, called royal jelly. During winter,
the colony stays in its hive and feeds on stored honey.

Cape Honeybee Facts

SUBSPECIES	*Apis mellifera capensis*
FAMILY	Bees
CLASS	Insects
SIZE	1–2 cm (0.4–0.8 in) long
RANGE	Southwestern South Africa in shrubland and farmland
DIET	Nectar and pollen

Some cells in a hive are used for housing eggs,
larvae, and pupae, while others are used for
storing pollen and honey.

A honeybee has two sets of wings, which are attached to each other by tiny hooks. At the tip of its abdomen, a female bee has an adapted egg-laying organ, called an ovipositor, which can inject venom to give a "sting."

Songbirds

Many shrubland birds are songbirds, also called oscines, a group of birds with a great variety of songs and calls. These small birds have anisodactyl feet—with three toes pointing forward and one backward—which are ideal for perching on branches. Shrubs provide cover for both birds and eggs.

GREATER DOUBLE-COLLARED SUNBIRD

This South African bird drinks nectar by reaching into flowers with its long, curving beak. It also eats insects and spiders, which are plucked from their web. The male has iridescent (shining in a rainbow of shades) feathers, which he shows off to attract a female by bobbing on a high branch.

RED-CAPPED ROBIN

Found in Australian shrubland, this species is named for its "cap" of red feathers. The male has a larger and brighter cap than the female, as well as a red belly. This bird perches on a low branch to watch for crawling beetles and ants—then pounces to seize them in its beak.

CHINESE WHITE-BROWED ROSEFINCH

This rosefinch's strong, cone-shaped beak is suited to grasping and cracking seeds. A male has a pink face and belly, while a female is brown, which helps her stay unnoticed while she sits on her nest. This is cup-shaped, hidden in a bush, and made of grass, twigs, and moss.

CYPRUS WARBLER

The Cyprus warbler is known for its fast, loud song, which it uses to communicate with its mate, to keep other warblers out of its territory, and perhaps just for pleasure. Females lay three to five eggs in a nest hidden in a bush or gorse thicket.

HOODED YELLOWTHROAT

The hooded yellowthroat lives in hillside shrubland in Mexico. It usually hides quietly in a thicket, but flutters to a high branch to sing when it wants to attract a mate. A female lays only two eggs, fewer than songbirds that must migrate to warmer regions in winter, since she is more likely to survive to lay eggs for several years.

WHITE-WINGED FAIRYWREN

Outside the mating season, all white-winged fairywrens have brown plumage that camouflages them among the saltbushes of Australian shrubland. In spring and summer, one male in each flock grows bright blue plumage and mates with several females, while the brown-feathered males help care for the chicks.

Songbird Facts

ORDER	Songbirds
CLASS	Birds
SIZE	6.5–70 cm (2.6–28 in) long
RANGE	All continents except Antarctica in all regions except polar ice
DIET	Seeds, fruits, nectar, insects, and other small animals

Desert

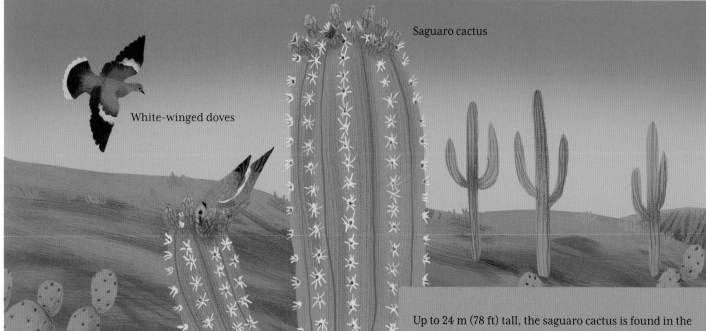

White-winged doves

Saguaro cactus

Up to 24 m (78 ft) tall, the saguaro cactus is found in the Sonoran Desert of the southwestern United States. It takes only one day of rainfall for the cactus's 30-m (100-ft) long root network to gather up to 750 l (165 gallons) of water and store it in its stem and branches. The cactus's fruit is a source of water and energy for animals including the white-winged dove.

A desert is an area with less than 25 cm (10 in) of rain per year. Some deserts are hot all year, with daytime temperatures over 54 °C (130 °F), but others have cold winters or are cold year-round. Deserts are in regions where the air holds little moisture because it has already fallen elsewhere as rain: in the middle of continents, far from the rain-bringing ocean; in the shadow of mountains; and in two bands around 2,000 km (1,240 miles) to the north and south of the equator. Deserts form in these bands because hot, damp air rises at the equator, drops its moisture as rain, then moves outward to the north and south, creating two areas of dry, cloudless air.

Since deserts have little rain, few plants can grow. With no covering of plants, the soil is blown away, leaving many deserts as rocky plains. When rock is battered by wind over thousands of years, it may break into sand, which can pile into dunes. Where plants are found, they usually have deep roots to reach underground moisture. They have small, hard leaves that release little water. Cacti are desert plants with leaves modified into spines that prevent animals reaching the water stored in their thick stem. Some plants grow from seed, bloom, and then die in the weeks after rainfall.

The few animals living in deserts must survive on little water. They get much of their water from eating plants

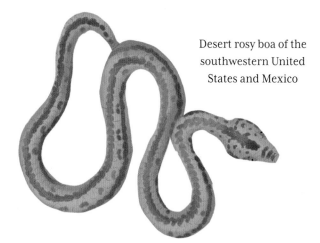

Desert rosy boa of the southwestern United States and Mexico

or from the blood of their prey. Some remain dormant during dry periods, sleeping deeply underground, then become active after rain. Many desert animals have a thick skin, so they lose little water to the air.

The temperature in East Asia's Gobi Desert reaches 45 °C (113 °F) on summer days, but it can fall to -47 °C (-53 °F) in winter. The Mongolian gerbil hides in its shared burrow during extremely hot and cold weather, as well as to escape predators such as the golden eagle. A member of the horse family, the onager gets most of its water from eating plants, but also digs for water in dry riverbeds using its hooves.

Sahara Desert

The world's largest hot desert, the Sahara covers 9.2 million sq km (3.6 million sq miles) of North Africa. Most of the region is rocky, but in sandy areas known as ergs, dunes soar to 180 m (590 ft) high. On summer days, the sand can be heated to 80 °C (176 °F).

In most of the Sahara Desert, the average daily temperature is more than 25 °C (77 °F). However, when the Sun sets, the lack of cloud cover means the air cools swiftly. Nights are always 13 to 20 °C (23 to 36 °F) cooler than days.

Many Saharan animals are nocturnal, staying in the shade or underground during the heat of day, then emerging at night to eat. Most are well camouflaged by dappled or sandy fur, feathers, or scales, which helps them go unnoticed among dunes and rocks.

FENNEC FOX

The smallest member of the dog family, this fox has huge ears. These help it stay cool because their large surface loses lots of body heat to the air. The fox's foot pads have thick fur to protect them from hot sand.

WEST AFRICAN CROCODILE

During dry periods, this crocodile digs a burrow and becomes dormant, sleeping so deeply that its body processes slow. After rain, it gathers with other crocodiles at a guelta, a pocket of water that collects in a valley.

DROMEDARY CAMEL

The dromedary stores fat in its hump, surviving on this energy for up to 2 months if it cannot find plants to eat. Thick eyebrows shade its eyes from sunlight, while long eyelashes protect them from wind-blown sand.

ADDAX

This antelope gets its water from plants and the dew that forms when the temperature drops at night. Cold air can hold less water than hot air, so droplets of dew collect on plants. The addax's pale fur reflects the Sun's heat so it stays cooler.

NORTHWEST AFRICAN CHEETAH

After sunset, this cheetah hunts antelopes, running at 100 km/h (62 miles per hour) as it gives chase. It can survive without drinking as long as it eats, since mammal blood is around 90 percent water.

DEATHSTALKER SCORPION

Up to 7.5 cm (3 in) long, the deathstalker has a curving tail ending in a sharp stinger that injects deadly venom into prey or predators. The scorpion's strong pincers are used for grasping and crushing prey such as insects and other scorpions.

Meerkat

This mammal lives in deserts and dry grasslands in southern Africa, including the Kalahari and Namib Deserts. It lives in a group of up to 40 meerkats, known as a mob or gang. The mob shares a burrow, inside which the temperature remains comfortable throughout the year.

MEERKAT MOB

In each meerkat mob, one pair of adults does the work of mating and giving birth. The other adults help care for the pair's pups. Mob members often groom and play with each other, which helps to maintain their friendships. Closeness between members of the mob is important, because meerkats rely on each other to watch for predators such as jackals, foxes, and eagles.

In the cool of early morning or late afternoon, a group of adults leaves the burrow to look for food. One of the adults climbs on a rock, stands tall on its back legs, and watches all around. The watching meerkat makes constant "peep" noises to tell the others that all is well. If danger is sighted, the watcher gives a high-pitched bark, and the mob runs into a burrow entrance.

BURROWING AND BATTLING

Each mob has several burrow systems within its territory. The mob moves from one burrow to another if the surrounding food is low. Up to 2 m (6.6 ft) deep, each burrow system has around 15 entrances and exits. When digging a burrow, meerkats scrape with their claws, scoop out the soil with their joined forepaws, then kick it behind with their back legs.

A mob defends its territory by marking the border with a strong-smelling liquid made in a gland beneath their tails. If another mob crosses this border, the mob puts on a threatening display to scare them away: leaping forward while kicking up their legs. If this show of strength fails, the meerkats will fight each other, which can result in injuries.

Meerkat Facts

SPECIES	*Suricata suricatta*
FAMILY	Mongooses
CLASS	Mammals
SIZE	40–60 cm (16–24 in) long
RANGE	Southern Africa in dry, treeless regions
DIET	Beetles, butterflies, scorpions, small birds, lizards, and plants

When a meerkat needs to warm up, it sunbathes on its back. The dark fur and skin of its belly soak up more warmth than its paler back.

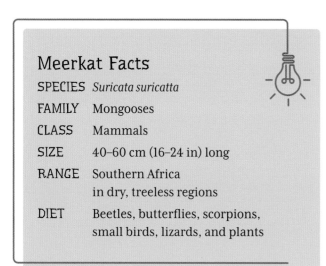

A group of adult meerkats searches for insects and plants to eat. A meerkat can survive without drinking water, because it gets the water it needs from eating plant roots and juicy fruits.

Snakes

Snakes are legless reptiles with wide-opening jaws for swallowing prey.
Some snakes make venom, a poison injected into prey with sharp, hollow fangs.
Other snakes swallow prey alive or kill prey by coiling tightly around it.
Snakes thrive in deserts, since they can last a long time without food and water.

NUBIAN SPITTING COBRA

Like all venomous snakes, the spitting cobra makes venom in glands behind its eyes. As well as injecting venom into prey, this snake defends itself by spraying venom from the front of its fangs, blinding an attacker if the venom enters the eyes. By squeezing muscles around its glands, the snake squirts venom up to 2 m (6.6 ft).

ARIZONA CORAL SNAKE

Unlike most desert snakes, which are shaded to blend in with desert sand, coral snakes are strikingly patterned. The easy-to-remember pattern warns that the snake is venomous, so predators, such as birds of prey, do not attack. This strategy is known as aposematism (from the ancient Greek for "away sign").

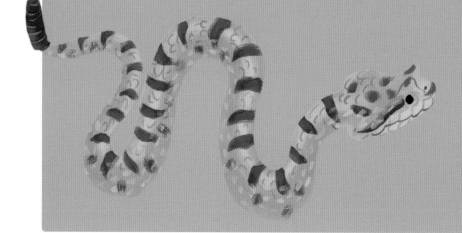

MOJAVE DESERT SIDEWINDER

This rattlesnake has a style of movement suited to slippery, shifting sand: sidewinding. It moves its body in a wave-like pattern, curving both vertically and sideways, which pushes it forward at a diagonal angle. To warn away predators, it shakes horny segments at the tip of its tail, making a rattling noise.

INLAND TAIPAN

Found in Australia, the inland taipan has the most powerful venom of any snake. The venom it injects with just one bite could kill 100 adult humans. However, this shy snake usually only bites small mammals, such as long-haired rats, which die almost instantly.

SAHARAN HORNED VIPER

This venomous snake lies partly buried in sand until birds or rodents approach—then it bites, holding prey in its mouth until the venom has taken effect. The tall scales above the snake's eyes, known as horns, may protect its eyes from blown sand.

DESERT ROSY BOA

Like most desert snakes, this snake changes its activities depending on the temperature. In the heat of summer, it spends the day beneath rocks. In the cooler night, it hunts for rats and mice, which it circles in its coils until they stop breathing. In winter, when the temperature falls in its North American home, the snake moves into a period of sleep and inactivity known as brumation.

Snake Facts

SUBORDER	Snakes
CLASS	Reptiles
SIZE	0.1–6.95 m (0.3–22.8 ft) long
RANGE	All continents except Antarctica; the Indian and Pacific Oceans
DIET	Lizards, frogs, small mammals, birds, eggs, fish, and invertebrates

Rain Forest

Emergent layer

Canopy

Understory

Forest floor

Harpy eagle

Hoffmann's two-toed sloth

Eyelash viper

Central American agouti

In the rain forest of Central America, a harpy eagle perches on an emergent tree, while a Hoffmann's two-toed sloth feeds on leaves in the canopy. In the understory, an eyelash viper waits for passing birds and frogs. A member of the rodent family, an agouti eats fallen fruit on the forest floor.

A rain forest is a region with lots of rain where many tall trees grow close together. Most of these trees are evergreens, which keep their leaves throughout the year. Although some rain forests are in temperate wet regions, the majority are in tropical regions, where hot, wet air brings at least 168 cm (66 in) of rain every year. The world's largest rain forests are in tropical South America, central Africa, and Southeast Asia.

Rain forests have four layers: emergent, canopy, understory, and forest floor. The top layer, known as the emergent layer, is where the tallest trees have their wobbling upper branches. Most animals here can fly or glide. Below is the canopy, a thick tangle of leaves and branches forming a roof over the two lower layers. With fruit and leaves to provide food, the canopy is busy with plant-eating animals from birds to primates such as monkeys. In the darker, drier understory, plants such as shrubs and vines have large leaves to catch as much sunlight as possible. Well-camouflaged animals such as frogs and snakes hide among the vegetation. Finally, on the dark forest floor, worms and insects eat rotting leaves, before becoming food for rodents and pangolins.

More than two-thirds of the world's animal and plant species live in rain forests, but this habitat is under threat. Trees are being cut down to make room for

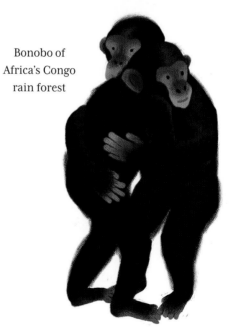

Bonobo of Africa's Congo rain forest

farming and industry, while loggers sell the wood for timber or fuel. Many people, charities, and governments are working to protect the rain forests and their animals.

In the rain forest of Africa's
Democratic Republic of the Congo,
a Congo peacock spreads his tail
feathers to attract a female, while
a long-tailed pangolin searches a
tree branch for ants. A relative of
the giraffe, an okapi uses its long,
muscular tongue to strip buds and
leaves from branches. All three
animals are threatened by the loss
of their habitat.

Amazon Rain Forest

The world's largest rain forest, the Amazon covers 5.5 million sq km (2.1 million sq miles) around South America's Amazon River. The forest is home to more than 1 million species of insects, 1,290 birds, 420 mammals, 420 amphibians, and 370 reptiles.

Brazil nut, kapok, and angelim trees are among the tallest emergent trees, growing up to 88.5 m (290 ft) high and living for hundreds of years. Many animals of the emergent layer have wings, including birds, bats, and butterflies.

In the thick canopy below, fruit-eating birds call loudly to communicate with each other through the screen of leaves. Hiding quietly in the dimly lit understory are hungry hunters and their prey, while plant- and insect-eaters snuffle through leaf litter on the forest floor.

WHITE-THROATED TOUCAN

Up to 60 cm (24 in) long, this bird uses its huge beak to reach for fruit as it sits on a tree branch. A toucan communicates with its flock using croaks, barks, and growls, as well as by clattering its beak.

AMAZON POISON DART FROG

Like most amphibians, this frog must lay its eggs in water, so the female deposits them in pools that collect in the leaves of bromeliad plants. The male watches over the tadpoles, sometimes carrying them to another bromeliad on his back. The frog's bright skin warns predators that it is poisonous.

SCARLET MACAW

This parrot grasps fruits, nuts, and insects with its large, hooked beak. It often flies in a squawking flock, with the bright patches on the birds' plumage making it hard for predators—such as eagles and hawks—to spot the outline of a single bird.

RHETENOR BLUE MORPHO

Measuring 10 cm (4 in) across, this butterfly's wings have bright blue uppersides and brown undersides. As the butterfly flaps, the flickering between blue and brown is hard for a butterfly-eating bird to focus on.

SOUTH AMERICAN TAPIR

This mammal uses it long, bendy, muscular snout to reach for shoots, leaves, fruit, and seeds. It often bathes in water or mud to stay cool and wash insects off its body.

JAGUAR

The jaguar is the Amazon's apex predator ("top hunter"), since it is too fierce to have predators of its own. It hides among the understory vegetation as it waits for an animal such as an anteater or tapir to pass—then it kills with a bite to the skull.

Southern Cassowary

Unable to fly, this bird grows to 1.8 m (5.9 ft) tall and weighs up to 70 kg (154 lb), about the same as an adult woman. It lives in rain forests in Australia, Papua New Guinea, and Indonesia, where it is known for being highly dangerous if it feels threatened.

LIFE ON THE GROUND

The southern cassowary, along with its relatives the northern and dwarf cassowaries, is a member of the ratite group of birds. This group includes ostriches, emus, rheas, and kiwis. Most ratites are flightless due to the weak muscles and bones in their breast and wings. They also have soft feathers that are not suited to pushing through the air in flight.

Yet the majority of ratites are large and have long, strong legs, which let them escape from predators by running. The southern cassowary can run at 50 km/h (30 miles per hour) and jump 2 m (6.6 ft) in the air. In addition, the inner toe on each of the cassowary's three-toed feet is armed with a knife-like claw up to 12 cm (4.7 in) long. The bird uses this claw to defend itself, by jumping, kicking, and slashing. However, the cassowary usually hides deep in the forest, where it feeds on fallen fruit and small animals.

CLEVER CASQUE

Like other cassowaries, the southern cassowary has a horny, skin-covered bump on its head known as a casque. This continues to grow through the cassowary's life, reaching 18 cm (7 in) tall. The inside of the casque is hollow but crossed by threadlike tissues. Scientists think that the casque makes the cassowary's calls louder, because the sounds bounce around inside the hollow chamber—like the hollow body of a guitar makes the sound of a plucked string louder. An adult cassowary, which usually lives alone, relies on its booming calls to find a mate in the thick rain forest.

Southern Cassowary Facts

SPECIES	*Casuarius casuarius*
FAMILY	Cassowaries and the emu
CLASS	Birds
SIZE	1.3–1.7 m (4.2–5.6 ft) long
RANGE	Papua New Guinea, Indonesia, and northern Australia
DIET	Fruit, mushrooms, insects, lizards, and mice

A female cassowary lays around four 14-cm- (5.5-in-) long eggs in a nest made by a male. The eggs are camouflaged on the forest floor by their green shells. The male cares for the eggs and chicks alone.

The cassowary plum tree takes its name from the cassowary, which is the only animal that eats its large purple fruits whole. When the bird poops, it plays the crucial role of spreading the seeds around the rain forest.

Primates

Around 55 million years ago, primates evolved in rain forests, where most still live today. Primates include monkeys, apes, lemurs, and humans. They are large-brained mammals that live in pairs or groups. Many live in trees, which they climb with the help of their strong limbs and grasping fingers and toes.

BORNEAN ORANGUTAN

Orangutans are in the great ape family, along with gorillas, chimpanzees, bonobos, and humans. Like other great apes, orangutans are tailless and clever, often using sticks to open fruit, poke termite nests, or catch fish. The Bornean orangutan is critically endangered due to the cutting down of its rain forest habitat.

LAR GIBBON

Although this gibbon's fur ranges from black to sandy, it always has a black, largely hairless face surrounded by white hair. It swings from branch to branch using its extremely long arms. On the rare times it comes to the ground, it walks on its short back legs while holding its arms over its head for balance.

RED-HANDED HOWLER MONKEY

This tree-dweller has a long tail that can curl around and hold branches, known as a prehensile tail. The howler communicates by making howling calls that can be heard up to 4.8 km (3 miles) away, the volume increased by an extra-large bone in the monkey's throat.

EMPEROR TAMARIN

The emperor tamarin was named for its white whiskers, which look like the mustache of German emperor Wilhelm II (1859–1941). This monkey eats fruit, flowers, frogs, and insects in the Amazon rain forest canopy. Both males and females help to carry, feed, and wash babies.

BONOBO

Along with the chimpanzee, the bonobo is humans' closest relative. It lives in the Congo rain forest, where it eats fruit, honey, eggs, and small mammals. Although bonobos sometimes fight, they also form lifelong friendships, share food, and hug each other when distressed.

BLACK-AND-WHITE RUFFED LEMUR

Living in the canopy of the Madagascan rain forest, this lemur feeds on fruit. Groups are led by females, which take the first choice of food, ensuring that they have enough energy to raise young. Females build their babies nests of leaves, where they care for them during their first weeks.

Primate Facts

ORDER	Primates
CLASS	Mammals
SIZE	0.2–1.7 m (0.6–5.6 ft) long (excluding humans)
RANGE	Nonhuman primates live in Central and South America, Africa, and southern Asia
DIET	Fruit, leaves, flowers, seeds, insects, and small mammals

Cities

House
centipede

Silverfish

Cities are busy human settlements with homes, stores, and workplaces. Roads crisscross cities and stretch to other cities and towns. Today, more than 500 cities have over 1 million inhabitants. More than 30 are megacities, which are home to over 10 million people. The world's earliest cities grew in western Asia around 7,000 years ago. Since then, animals have been driven from—or learned to adapt to—these human-made habitats.

Animals with particular diet and habitat needs can be driven to extinction by growing cities, as their food and shelter disappear. Even when portions of an animal's habitat remain, it may be divided into smaller areas by roads. Known as habitat fragmentation, this can prevent animals from migrating to find food or mates. Pollution from cities can also endanger animals, such as the axolotl, an amphibian driven close to extinction by loss of its lake habitat and water pollution in Mexico City.

However, some animals with varied diet and habitat needs can do well in cities. Many wild animals survive in the limited green spaces found in cities, such as city forests, parks, yards, and gardens. These animals, including birds, insects, and spiders, may have little or no contact with humans. Yet some wild animals actually benefit from living around humans and in human-made habitats, such as homes and garbage dumps.

Silverfish are wingless insects that live in most of the world's cities, where they can be found in bathrooms, attics, basements, and kitchens. They feed on books, photos, carpets, clothing, hair, coffee, and sugar. Silverfish are preyed on by house centipedes, which can climb up walls and across ceilings on up to 15 pairs of legs.

Splendid peacock spider of Sydney in Australia

These animals, known as synanthropes (from the ancient Greek for "together with humans"), get shelter and easy-to-find food that allow them to thrive. Some synanthropes, such as house mice, are able to expand their range into colder regions where they could not survive away from the warmth of cities.

Japan's busy capital city, Tokyo is home to 14 million people, but—after darkness falls—wild animals come out of hiding in its parks, temple gardens, and quieter streets. A nocturnal member of the dog family, the tanuki searches for insects, slugs, rodents, and fruit. Overhead, the Japanese house bat leaves its roost under the roof of an old building, closely followed by a hungry Japanese scops owl.

New York City

New York is the United States' biggest city, with more than 8 million human inhabitants. New Yorkers share their parks, streets, and homes with wild animals from crawling bugs to soaring birds of prey.

Some of New York's animals are considered pests, which are animals that are harmful or annoying for humans to find in their bedroom or kitchen. New York pests include rodents, which may carry diseases, and tiny, biting invertebrates such as fleas and bedbugs.

Yet plenty of New York's animals, including its many birds, are helpful to humans. Birds of prey—such as the peregrine falcon, American kestrel, and red-tailed hawk—feed on pests, while the calls of songbirds are enjoyed in parks and yards.

RACCOON
These mammals eat waste, pet food, dead animals, birds, insects, and squirrels. Flexible fingers help them open garbage cans and bird feeders.

COMMON PIGEON

The city's million or more pigeons are descended from domestic pigeons that have returned to the wild. Kept by humans for food and carrying messages, domestic pigeons were bred from wild common pigeons, which are native to parts of Europe, Africa, and Asia.

RED-TAILED HAWK

This large bird of prey builds its nest on roofs, fire escapes, bridges, or trees. From a high perch, it watches for prey—such as pigeons, mice, and squirrels—then swoops to snatch its victim with its sharp claws.

STRIPED SKUNK

This mammal sleeps in a burrow in grassy areas, including New York's Central Park. To drive away an attacker, the skunk sprays a stinking liquid made in glands under its tail.

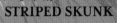

BROWN RAT

New York is home to around 2 million rats, many of them brown rats, which were originally from East Asia but have spread across the world. Rats live in groups of up to 50 in buildings and sewers, feeding on waste food and insects.

AMERICAN COCKROACH

Native to Africa, this insect was spread to the Americas on board ships. It lives in damp places such as sewers, pipes, and basements. Preferred foods include books, flakes of human skin, cheese, beer, and tea.

Red Fox

This member of the dog family is common in European, Asian, North American, and Australian cities, as well as grassland, forests, and mountains. City red foxes grow larger than their country relatives due to finding plenty of food and few predators.

CITY LIFE

In cities, red foxes are most common in suburban areas with yards and gardens in which to dig a burrow, known as a den, where they can store food, escape danger, and give birth. However, red foxes also live in the heart of cities, where they make dens in parks and the undergrowth beside rail tracks.

City foxes take food from garbage bags and bins, as well as hunting for pigeons, mice, insects, worms, berries, and vegetables. They usually avoid pet cats and dogs because of their large size and confidence. Red foxes do most of their hunting in the dim light of late evening and early morning. When not hunting for food, they often sleep among thick undergrowth close to their den, but will go inside the den to avoid bad weather. On sunny days, they may be seen sunbathing on lawns and the roofs of sheds. However, they should not be approached as they carry disease.

FOX FAMILY

Red foxes usually live with their mate and their young, known as kits. An adult female gives birth in the family den every spring. The average litter is four to six kits. Newborn kits are toothless, blind, and deaf. They drink their mother's milk while huddling close to her to stay warm.

After 3 or 4 weeks, kits can bite, see, and hear, so they venture outside the den and try solid food brought by their parents. Some red foxes leave their parents when they reach adulthood at around 9 to 10 months' old, but others stay and help care for younger kits.

A red fox kit is born with blue eyes, which change to orange-brown by 5 weeks' old. Its fur is brown, which gives better camouflage around the den than the red adult coat.

Red Fox Facts

SPECIES *Vulpes vulpes*

FAMILY Dogs

CLASS Mammals

SIZE 0.75–1.45 m (2.5–4.8 ft) long

RANGE North America, Europe, North Africa, Asia, and Australia

DIET Waste food, small mammals, birds, insects, worms, and fruit

The red fox's large, upright ears help to channel sounds into its ear canal. It can hear a squeaking mouse from around 100 m (330 ft) away.

Spiders

Spiders belong to a group of invertebrates known as arachnids, which have a two-part body and eight legs. Spiders also have silk-making organs and hollow fangs that can inject venom. In cities, some spiders grow particularly large due to the warmth and quantity of small prey.

ZEBRA JUMPING SPIDER

Rather than spinning a web to catch prey, this spider follows small invertebrates—then pounces on them. It has two large front eyes and six smaller eyes to help it spot, track, and judge the distance to prey. Around 5 to 9 mm (0.2 to 0.4 in) long, this spider lives in yards and homes in North America, Europe, and North Asia.

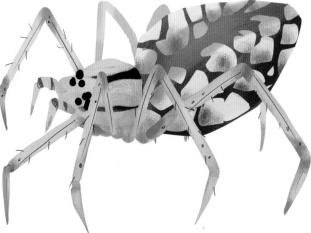

MIRROR SPIDER

This tiny spider is found in yards and gardens in the Southeast Asian city of Singapore. Like all spiders, its body has two parts: the cephalothorax, on which are its eyes, mouthparts, and legs; and the abdomen, which contains its heart, stomach, and silk-making organs. Its abdomen has patches that reflect sunlight, making this spider difficult for predators to spot.

REDBACK SPIDER

Female redbacks often build their untidy silk webs in human homes in Australia. When insects are tangled in the web, females give a venomous bite, wrap them in silk, then suck out their insides. Males, which are smaller, live on the edges of a female's web and steal leftovers. Redback bites are dangerous to humans, but they can be treated by antivenom.

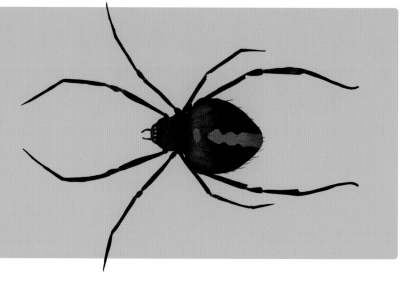

SPLENDID PEACOCK SPIDER

Male peacock spiders have a fan of bright scales and hairs on their abdomen, which they display to attract a female. In contrast, females have a brown abdomen, so they are camouflaged among leaves and branches. These spiders grow just 5 mm (0.2 in) long.

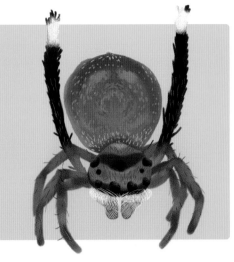

HUMPED GOLDEN ORB WEAVER

This spider is named for the golden glimmer of its silken webs. These attract bees, which like yellow because many flowers are yellow. The spider is common in yards and parks in Australian cities, where it grows bigger and lays more eggs than in wild habitats.

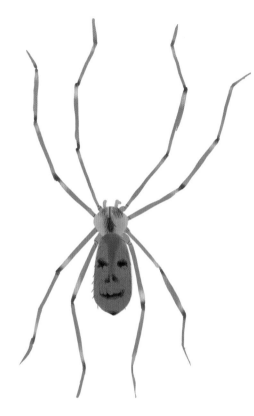

DADDY LONG-LEGS SPIDER

This spider's body is 8 mm (0.3 in) long, but its legs are up to 48 mm (1.9 in) long. Its abdomen has markings that look like a human skull, giving it the alternative name of skull spider. The species is from warm regions of Asia, but has been accidentally spread around the world by humans. In colder regions, it prefers the warmth of human homes.

Spider Facts

ORDER	Spiders
CLASS	Arachnids
SIZE	0.04–13 cm (0.02–5.1 in) long (excluding legs)
RANGE	All continents except Antarctica in all regions except polar ice
DIET	Insects, arachnids, plants, lizards, frogs, fish, mice, and birds

Wetland

Nymphaea
water lily

Northern jacana

The northern jacana lives in marshes and swamps of Central America, Mexico, and the Caribbean. Its long toes and claws spread its weight, so that it can walk across lily pads in search of insects, snails, worms, and crabs.

Wetlands are found on every continent except Antarctica. They are areas of land that are covered by water either constantly or for some of the time. Wetlands lie along the border between dry land and bodies of water, such as springs, rivers, lakes, and oceans. The water that covers a wetland may by salty sea water, unsalted fresh water, or a mixture of the two, known as brackish water, which is found along coasts. Water-living plants, known as aquatic plants, grow in a wetland.

Different types of wetlands are often named for their source of water. Tidal wetlands are flooded at high tide, when the ocean rises up the shore once or twice a day. Floodplains are low-lying areas that are flooded when water overflows from rivers and lakes. Wetlands are also named for their types of aquatic plants. In a marsh, most plants are low grasses, rushes, and reeds. In a swamp, most plants are water-tolerant trees. In bogs and fens, dead plant material, known as peat, has built up on the ground.

Some animals spend all their life in wetlands, while others are found in wetlands during only part of their life cycle. Wetlands offer shelter and plenty of food, so they are often mating grounds for fish and amphibians. Birds use wetlands for feeding, nesting, and as stopovers on their migration routes. Wetland mammals, reptiles, and

Southern leopard frog of
eastern North America

invertebrates have features that help them thrive in a wet habitat, from waterproof fur to webbed feet for wading or swimming.

France's marshy Camargue wetland lies where the Rhône River meets the Mediterranean Sea. The region's Camargue horse has extra-hard, wide hooves that prevent it from sinking into soggy ground. Flocks of greater flamingos wade on their long legs, sucking muddy water through their beak to trap shrimp and algae. Young goblet-marked damselflies live in the water, but winged adults perch on reeds as they watch for insects to catch.

Sundarbans

On the India–Bangladesh border, on the low-lying land where the Ganges and Brahmaputra Rivers snake to the Indian Ocean, is the Sundarbans. This vast swamp wetland is the meeting point of land, fresh water, and sea water.

The Sundarbans is home to the world's largest mangrove swamp, where mangrove trees live in salty, brackish, and fresh water, their stilt-like roots keeping their leaves above the tide. Countless streams and ocean inlets surround areas of muddy ground, known as mudflats.

The tangled roots of mangroves provide a safe place to lay eggs for both ocean and freshwater fish, as well as crabs and other invertebrates. More than 290 bird species live in the wetland or migrate here to spend the winter. Over 42 mammal, 35 reptile, and 8 amphibian species make the Sundarbans their permanent home.

FISHING CAT

The fishing cat hunts for fish by leaning over the water to grab with its clawed paws—or by diving right in. After swimming, it dries itself quickly by shaking off its thick, waterproof fur.

NORTHERN RIVER TERRAPIN

This reptile spends most of its life in water, but it climbs onto a bank or log to warm up in sunshine. At mating time, the skin of the male's neck and front legs flushes bright pink to attract a female's attention.

BLACK-CAPPED KINGFISHER

This kingfisher perches on a branch over the water. When it spots fish, it swoops to snatch them with its long, wide beak. At low tide, it seizes small crabs exposed on the mudflats.

BARRED MUDSKIPPER

Unlike most of its relatives, this fish can survive out of water for many hours. It lives in a burrow on mudflats, where it catches crabs. It "skips" across the mud using its pectoral (side) fins like legs. Most fish can only take in oxygen from water using their gills, but—as long as the mudskipper stays damp—it can also soak up oxygen from the air through its skin.

BARRAMUNDI

A female barramundi lays up to 32 million eggs among the mangroves each year. When the young fish hatch, they find plenty of tiny animals, larvae, and eggs to eat in the warm, sheltered water.

MANGROVE HORSESHOE CRAB

Despite its name, this invertebrate is more closely related to spiders than to crabs. Protected by its hard shell, it crawls across the muddy water bottom searching for insect larvae, which it grinds up using the bristles on its legs since it does not have jaws.

American Alligator

The American alligator is an apex predator in freshwater marshes and swamps in the southeastern United States. It belongs to an order of large, strong reptiles known as crocodilians, which also includes crocodiles, caimans, and gharials.

ALLIGATOR LIFE

Like other crocodilians, the American alligator spends part of its life on land and part in water, where it swims by swinging its muscular tail. It hunts both in water and on land—and will even jump up to 1.5 m (5 ft) into the air to reach birds. The alligator's long snout contains up to 80 sharp, cone-shaped teeth, which give one of the most powerful bites of any animal. Its bite force is more than 13,000 Newtons, with 1 Newton being the force needed to throw a weight of 1 kg (2.2 lb) a distance of 1 m (3.3 ft) in 1 second.

A female American alligator lays 20 to 50 eggs in a nest built from leaves and mud near water. She covers the eggs with leaves, which heat as they rot, keeping the eggs warm. Eggs kept at between 32.5 °C and 33.5 °C (90.5 °F and 92.3 °F) will produce males, while cooler or hotter eggs produce females. The female stays nearby to protect the eggs until they hatch.

A KEY ANIMAL

The American alligator is known as a keystone species, which is an animal that has a great effect on the other animals in its habitat. This is partly because the alligator is the largest predator in its habitat, but also because it makes important changes to the habitat. Using its feet and snout, the alligator digs ponds known as alligator holes. Water remains in these ponds in the dry season, so the alligator can stay cool. Yet the ponds also provide a place for small water-living animals—such as fish, turtles, and frogs—to survive the dry season, although some also become food for the alligator.

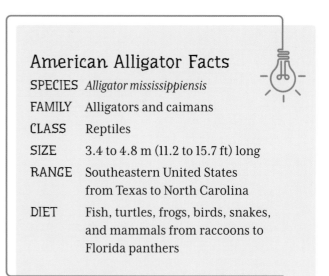

American Alligator Facts

SPECIES	*Alligator mississippiensis*
FAMILY	Alligators and caimans
CLASS	Reptiles
SIZE	3.4 to 4.8 m (11.2 to 15.7 ft) long
RANGE	Southeastern United States from Texas to North Carolina
DIET	Fish, turtles, frogs, birds, snakes, and mammals from raccoons to Florida panthers

A young alligator, called a hatchling, will remain with its mother for up to 2 years.

The American alligator rests
on a log or bank to warm
itself in the sunshine after
swimming. Its tough skin
is protected by bony plates
covered with horn.

Frogs

These amphibians have large eyes, long back legs suited to jumping, and no tail.
They usually lay their eggs in fresh water. Young frogs, known as tadpoles, live in water.
Most adult frogs live on land but stay close to fresh water or inhabit damp forests.

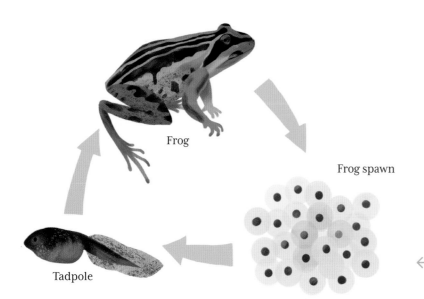

Frog

Frog spawn

Tadpole

STRIPED MARSH FROG

Like nearly all frogs, the striped marsh frog goes through changes known as metamorphosis. Eggs, known as frog spawn, are laid in a pond or ditch. After hatching, the tadpoles have a tail and no legs. They swim in the water, feed on algae, and take oxygen from water using body parts called gills. Over several months, the tadpoles grow legs, lose their tail, and develop lungs for taking oxygen from air. Their mouth grows wider for eating insects and slugs.

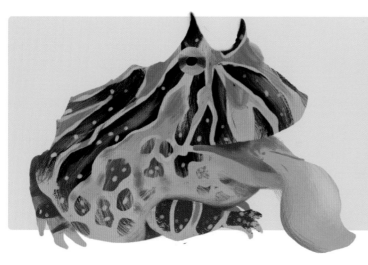

BRAZILIAN HORNED FROG

Using its strong, sticky tongue, this 30-cm- (12-in-) long frog grabs prey as large as mice. Its wide mouth has sharp teeth in the upper jaw. The frog's leaflike horns and green-yellow pattern help it hide in marshes and wet leaves. Its bulky body and short legs make it a slow crawler rather than a speedy hopper.

MADAGASCAR TOMATO FROG

Named for its red skin, this frog is found in marshes, swamps, and ponds. Its bright shade warns predators that it is poisonous, since venom seeps from its skin. When threatened, this frog also puffs up its body, making itself more frightening and more difficult to swallow.

INDIAN BULLFROG

Up to 17 cm (6.7 in) long, this frog often lives in holes in flooded rice fields. In the mating season, the skin of male Indian bullfrogs changes from olive green to bright yellow, with blue vocal sacs. The sound of the male's mating calls bounces around inside these elastic throat sacs, making them louder. Brighter, louder males find more mates.

ISHIKAWA'S TORRENT FROG

Most wetland frogs are found around still or slow-moving water, but this Japanese frog lives around swift-flowing mountain streams and waterfalls. It lays its eggs on wet, mossy rocks on the banks. The tadpoles stay in the safety of rock pools, so that they are not washed away.

SOUTHERN LEOPARD FROG

This nocturnal frog lives around ponds, swamps, and flooded caves and mines in North America. Only 9 cm (3.5 in) long, its strong back legs let it jump up to 90 cm (3 ft). Females lay 1,500 eggs on water plants, often in a mass with the eggs of other females to keep them warm.

Frog Facts

ORDER	Frogs
CLASS	Amphibians
SIZE	0.7–32 cm (0.3–12.6 in) long
RANGE	All continents except Antarctica but absent from some isolated islands
DIET	Insects, worms, snails, frogs, mice, and snakes

Shores

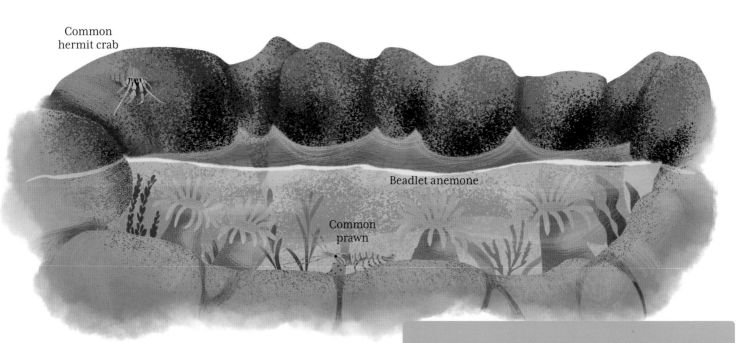

Common hermit crab

Beadlet anemone

Common prawn

At low tide, a tide pool is cut off from the ocean. On the Atlantic Coast of Europe, a tide pool's inhabitants include a common prawn and a sea anemone, which catches small creatures with its stinging tentacles. Not a true crab, a hermit crab lives inside the discarded shell of a sea snail.

The shore is where an ocean or lake meets the land. The nature of a shore depends on the rock and soil along the coast, as well as how waves crash or lap against them. Beaches are gently sloping areas covered by mud or by rock, shells, or coral that have been broken into pebbles or tinier grains of sand then dropped by gentle waves. Cliffs are steep rock walls formed by powerful waves crashing against the shore, wearing away the rock until it crumbles and falls.

There are three zones along ocean shores. The lowest is the subtidal zone, which is always below water but is close enough to shore for its animals and plants to be buffeted by the constant pounding and pulling of waves. The middle zone is the intertidal zone, which is below water at high tide but exposed to air, wind, and sunlight when the water draws out at low tide. The highest zone is the sea spray zone, which is never below the tide but is sprayed by salty water. Usually only tough, low-growing plants—as well as plantlike algae, such as seaweeds—can survive in these zones.

Shore-dwelling animals must thrive in harsh and constantly changing conditions. When the tide rises, most birds move higher up the shore, while some fly far inland in the face of ocean storms. Some hard-shelled invertebrates, such as mussels and barnacles, cling to

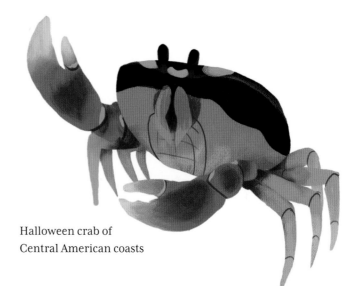

Halloween crab of Central American coasts

rocks so they are not dragged out to sea. At low tide, many invertebrates burrow into the sand or hide among seaweed to stay damp.

The fish-eating Atlantic puffin nests in burrows on the cliffs of Wales' Puffin Island, where few predators can reach its eggs. Below, in the intertidal zone, a common starfish preys on a blue mussel by pulling open the shell with its arms, pushing its stomach (on its underside) into the shell, breaking down the mussel's soft body with stomach juices, then pulling back its stomach.

Victory Beach

New Zealand's Victory Beach is named for the steamship *Victory*, which ran aground here in 1861. Visited by several endangered animals, the sandy beach is backed by dunes where pikao sedge and marram grass grow, while seaweeds such as bull kelp are washed ashore.

Victory Beach is a mating ground for birds and mammals, such as penguins and sea lions, that spend much of their life at sea but must return to land to lay eggs or give birth. Some shorebirds make the beach their permanent home. These birds have long legs for wading through shallow water and webbed feet so they do not sink into soft sand.

Many invertebrates here are burrowers, which gives protection from being washed away by waves or attacked by predators such as birds. These invertebrates usually have a regular pattern of burrowing and emerging to feed that matches the rising and falling of the tides.

PIED STILT

Named for its long, stilt-like legs, this bird feeds in shallow water, using its long, pointed beak to dig into sand for invertebrates. It nests on the ground among sand, pebbles, or grasses, where its eggs are camouflaged by yellow-brown blotchy shells.

ROYAL SPOONBILL

Also known by the Maori name *kotuku ngutupapa*, this long-legged wading bird feeds by swinging its partly open, spoon-shaped beak from side to side in shallow water. When it feels fish, shellfish, or crabs, it snaps them up.

NEW ZEALAND SEA LION

This sea lion is endangered due to habitat loss and past hunting. Females come ashore to give birth, then walk their pups up to 2 km (1.2 miles) to inland forests to protect them from storms. Unlike seals, sea lions can walk on all fours by turning their back flippers forward.

YELLOW-EYED PENGUIN

This New Zealand penguin is endangered due to predators, such as cats, which were brought to the islands by humans. Unlike Antarctic penguins, which nest in large colonies, a pair of yellow-eyed penguins nests out of sight of others.

LUGWORM

The lugworm makes the worm-shaped coils of sand often seen on beaches. These coils are formed by the burrowing lugworm swallowing sand—to catch the tiny animals and waste it contains—and then pooping it out.

SANDHOPPER

Up to 2 cm (0.8 in) long, this jumping invertebrate spends the daytime buried in damp sand or in seaweed washed up on shore. It comes out at night to feed on decaying seaweed.

Marine Iguana

Found on the Pacific Ocean's Galápagos Islands, the marine iguana is the world's only lizard that spends time in the ocean. It usually lives on a rocky shore in a colony of 20 to 500 or even 1,000 iguanas, but it is sometimes seen on sandy beaches or in mangrove swamps.

EATING ALGAE

The marine iguana eats algae, which are simple, plantlike living things that grow in water. Often known as seaweeds, algae are found as carpet-like beds or frondy stems. Adult marine iguanas feed on algae growing in the intertidal and subtidal zones. Females and small males feed on algae that grows only just offshore or is exposed at low tide. Large males, which have more powerful limbs and bigger lungs, will dive up to 30 m (98 ft) deep to feed, spending up to an hour underwater before they swim to the surface for air.

In the first few months of life, young marine iguanas mainly eat the poop of adults. By doing so, they take in bacteria that lives in the adults' guts and helps them to digest tough algae.

A large male marine iguana swims by waving its flattened tail, while pulling itself over seafloor rocks with its long, sharp claws. It has heavier bones than a land iguana, which helps it dive to the bottom.

SUITED TO ITS HABITAT

This lizard's short, blunt nose and sharp teeth let it chew off algae that is growing on rocks. During feeding, the iguana takes in salt from the water and from algae. Too much salt would damage the iguana's organs, so it is filtered from the blood by special glands in the nostrils, then sneezed out of the body.

Like other reptiles, the marine iguana cannot make its own body heat. The sea around the Galápagos Islands is fairly cold, around 11 °C to 23 °C (52 °F to 73 °F), so the iguana warms itself in a sunny spot between swims. The iguana has dark skin, which soaks up more warmth than pale skin (which reflects more sunlight than it absorbs). The row of spikes on the iguana's back soaks up sunshine easily. To stay warm at night, most marine iguanas huddle together, but some shelter between rocks or under plants.

A male marine iguana's skin turns pink during the mating season.

Marine Iguana Facts

SPECIES *Amblyrhynchus cristatus*

FAMILY Iguanas

CLASS Reptiles

SIZE 0.3 to 1.4 m (1 to 4.6 ft) long

RANGE Galápagos Islands in the Pacific Ocean

DIET Algae, poop, and small invertebrates

Crabs

There are around 4,500 species of crabs, which are decapod ("ten-footed") invertebrates. Crabs have a hard shell called an exoskeleton. They have eight walking legs, plus two front legs that end in pincers. Usually living in or around water, crabs can often be seen on shorelines.

RED ROCK CRAB

An inhabitant of rocky seashores, a female red rock crab carries her eggs on her body, stuck beneath her tail flap. When the spiny larvae hatch, she releases them into the ocean. After the larvae grow into young adults, they swim ashore. Young adults are black, keeping them camouflaged among rocks. As they grow, they shed their shell whenever it becomes too small, revealing a new, brighter shell beneath.

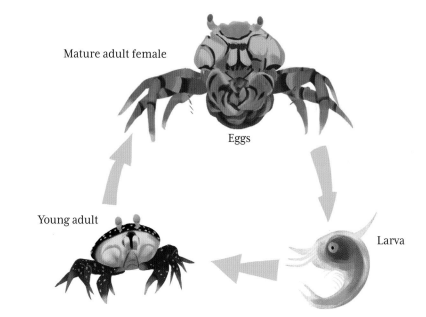

Mature adult female

Eggs

Larva

Young adult

VELVET SWIMMING CRAB

Named for its covering of short hairs, which looks like velvet, this crab can be recognized by its red eyes. It lives in tide pools and shallow water, where it swims using its flattened, paddle-like back legs. With its strong, sharp pincers, it seizes prey such as fish and prawns.

NORTHERN KELP CRAB

The northern kelp crab lives in the intertidal zone, in the area of shore that is above water at low tide and under water at high tide. It feeds on kelp and other seaweeds. Its shell has hook-shaped bristles, on which it sticks kelp so it can eat when it chooses.

ELEGANT FIDDLER CRAB

Male fiddler crabs have one pincer much larger than the other. The large pincer is used for fighting with other males. Females choose a mate with a big pincer that he can wave vigorously. These are signs that he is healthy and will dig a large burrow where the female can lay eggs.

HALLOWEEN CRAB

The Halloween crab digs a burrow among mangroves, sand dunes, or coastal rain forest in Central America. At night, it emerges to hunt for leaves to eat, climbing tree trunks to grasp twigs in its claws. It carries food back to its burrow, so it can eat in safety.

ATLANTIC GHOST CRAB

This well-camouflaged crab lives in a burrow that it digs with its pincers on a sandy seashore. It swivels its stalked eyes to keep a lookout. The crab enters the water only to release its larvae or moisten its gills. Like all crabs, it breathes through gills, which must be damp to soak up oxygen.

Crab Facts

INFRAORDER	Crabs
ORDER	Decapods
SIZE	0.01–3.7 m (0.03–12.1 ft) long
RANGE	All oceans plus land and fresh water of all continents except Antarctica
DIET	Algae, plants, invertebrates, fish, and waste

Coastal Ocean

Usually found in shallow coastal waters, the West Indian manatee is a mammal distantly related to elephants. It uses its flexible snout for grasping seagrass to eat.

The coastal ocean is shallow sea water close to land. Lit by sunlight, this water is home to plants and algae, which need sunlight to make their food. These plants include seagrasses, which have grasslike leaves. Underwater meadows of seagrass are found from polar coastal waters to tropical regions. Forests of kelp, a type of algae, grow in polar and temperate coastal waters. Coral reefs can often be found in shallow, clear tropical waters. Coral reefs are underwater structures built by colonies of tiny animals called coral polyps. Reef-building corals need sunlight because they get much of their energy from tiny algae that live within them. The algae use sunlight to make sugar for energy, which they share with their host.

Around 90 percent of all ocean animals live in the coastal ocean, within around 230 km (143 miles) of land. Plants, algae, and coral provide food for many ocean animals, as well as hiding places for prey and predators alike. Many fish and invertebrates, such as shrimp, lay their eggs in these sheltered areas, before swimming farther from land.

Coastal waters are also the ocean region most at risk from human activities. These waters are affected by pollution from factories, farms, and cities. Construction along the coast can damage habitats and create noise or light that disrupts animals. The coastal ocean is also

Great hammerhead shark of the coastal Atlantic, Indian, and Pacific Oceans

where much fishing takes place. Some fishing methods, such as overfishing and dragging nets, can be harmful. Overfishing is when too many fish in one species are caught, leaving the remaining fish unable to reproduce quickly enough to keep up their numbers.

More than 20 species of kelp grow from the seafloor off the coast of California, in the United States. The tallest kelps reach more than 30 m (100 ft) tall and form a canopy that covers the ocean surface. Sea otters wrap themselves in kelp so they do not drift as they nap. In the water below, the red octopus hunts for prey such as the jeweled top snail, which feeds on the kelp itself.

Red Sea Reef

Lying between the continents of Africa and Asia, the Red Sea is an inlet of the Indian Ocean. In the warm, shallow waters along its coasts are around 2,000 km (1,240 miles) of coral reef, which are home to about 200 species of coral and more than 1,200 fish species.

The Red Sea's warm, clear water makes it ideal for reef-building corals. The sea is one of the world's warmest bodies of sea water, with an average summer surface temperature of 28 °C (82 °F) and a winter temperature of 22 °C (72 °F).

However, the reef is at risk from global warming, which is causing a worldwide rise in sea temperatures. When the water gets hotter than 30 °C (86 °F), the coral polyps become stressed and expel the algae from which they get much of their energy. This results in an event known as coral bleaching, when the coral turns white, is weakened, and may fall victim to disease.

SOFTCORAL SEAHORSE

This fish curls its tail around coral while it waits for small prey to pass—then sucks hard through its long snout. A female seahorse lays her eggs in a pouch on the male's belly. When the babies hatch, the male "gives birth" by squeezing them out of his pouch.

FINGER CORAL

This coral and its relatives build much of the stone-like structure of the reef. Living in a colony of many thousands, each polyp builds a hard skeleton around its soft body, one on top of the other, forming a single branching structure. Each polyp, around 2 mm (0.08 in) across, extends tentacles to catch tiny floating animals.

ROYAL ANGELFISH

Like many reef fish, the angelfish has a body that is narrow from side to side, which helps it to change direction quickly and to swim through crevices. Its bold pattern is camouflage on the sunlight-dappled reef as it breaks up the fish's body shape, making it harder to spot.

BIGHORN NUDIBRANCH

This sea slug's bright patterns warn predators that it tastes nasty, due to the fact it feeds only on foul-tasting sea squirts (pictured). On the slug's back are red, branching gills that soak up oxygen from the water.

PURPLESTREAK PARROTFISH

Named for its parrot-like beak, this fish eats algae it scrapes off coral and rocks. As it feeds, it also bites off rock, which it poops as sand. A large parrotfish can produce up to 90 kg (200 lb) of sand per year. Most parrotfish start life as female but change to male as they age.

CHRISTMAS TREE WORM

After anchoring itself on a *Porites* coral, this worm builds a hard tube into which it can pull its body for protection. When feeding, the worm extends two feathery, tentacled structures that resemble Christmas trees. These trap tiny prey, then transport it to the worm's mouth.

Green Sea Turtle

This reptile has paddle-like limbs, a beaklike mouth, and a body covered by a strong shell called a carapace. It can stay underwater for up to 2 hours before swimming to the surface to breathe. It is usually found in warm, shallow coastal waters, where it feeds on seagrasses.

An adult green sea turtle rips seagrasses using the hard, jagged edge of its beak.

ALL IN THE NAME

The green sea turtle gets its name from the green body fat found under an adult's carapace. This fat is tinged green by the turtle's diet of seagrasses. However, young sea turtles live in deeper waters, where they feed on animals such as jellyfish, crabs, and worms. The different diets of young and adult turtles may be helpful in preventing competition for food.

A LONG LIFE

Green sea turtles live for up to 80 years. They are mature enough to mate when they reach around 25 years old. In time for the mating season, adult male and female sea turtles return to the shallow water near the beach

where they were born. This may mean a journey of up to 2,600 km (1,600 miles) between the turtle's feeding and mating sites. Yet this journey is worthwhile because the turtles know they will find a mate and a warm, sandy beach suitable for egg-laying. Scientists think that turtles find their way by sensing Earth's magnetic field, since the planet's iron-rich core makes it a magnet with a north and south pole.

When a female is ready to lay eggs, she uses her back flippers to dig a hole on the beach, in a dry spot above the high tide. After laying up to 200 eggs, she buries them with sand. She may make up to five such nests in each mating season, before swimming back to her feeding site.

After 50 to 70 days, the eggs hatch all at once during the night. The baby turtles, called hatchlings, climb out of the sand and make their way to the water, instinctively knowing which direction to take. Despite the darkness, this is a dangerous journey, since predators such as gulls and crabs may be watching.

A green turtle hatchling is around 5 cm (2 in) long. Only around one in every hundred is likely to live to maturity.

Green Sea Turtle Facts

SPECIES	*Chelonia mydas*
FAMILY	Sea turtles
CLASS	Reptiles
SIZE	0.9 to 1.5 m (3 to 4.9 ft) long
RANGE	Warm regions of the Atlantic, Indian, and Pacific Oceans
DIET	Seagrasses, algae, small invertebrates, and fish eggs

Sharks

Sharks are fish that—unlike most fish—have a skeleton made of bendy cartilage rather than bone. Nearly all sharks are hunters that track down prey using their keen senses. Some sharks swim in the open ocean, but others hunt in shallow water where there is plenty of food.

SIXGILL SAWSHARK

Sharks breathe by letting water flow into their mouth and through their gills, which soak up the water's oxygen. Water flows out of sharks' gill slits, on the sides of their body. Unlike most sharks, which have five gill slits, this shark has six. It also has a long, saw-like snout called a rostrum, with which it hits fish and stirs up sand in search of shrimp and crabs.

BLACKTIP REEF SHARK

Named for the black tips to its fins, this shark lives on coral reefs in the Pacific and Indian Oceans. Unlike most fish, which lay eggs, this shark gives birth to live young, called pups. The pups stay in very shallow water close to shore, where large predators cannot swim.

GREAT WHITE SHARK

Up to 6.1 m (20 ft) long, this shark has a sense of smell so powerful that it can smell one drop of blood in 10 billion drops of water. With its strong, flexible jaws, it can seize prey as large as seals and dolphins. It has 300 jagged-edged teeth arranged in rows, so when a front tooth falls out, the tooth behind moves forward to take its place.

GREAT HAMMERHEAD SHARK

The heads of sharks are dotted with tiny organs called ampullae of Lorenzini, which detect the electric charges given off by all animals as they move. Due to this shark's hammer-shaped head, its ampullae cover a wider area, so it can sense the movements even of prey buried in sand.

HORN SHARK

This small shark has a sharp spine at the front of each of its two dorsal (back) fins. If attacked, the horn shark jabs with its spines. The shark spends much of its time on the seafloor, where its big nostrils help it smell prey and its large, high eyes can see over surrounding coral.

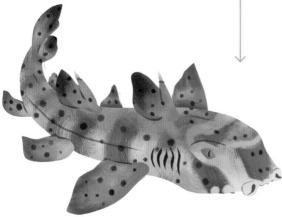

BANDED WOBBEGONG

This flat-bodied shark lies motionless among coral, where it is camouflaged by its blotchy skin and fringe of algae-like skin flaps. The flaps also have sensitive cells that help the shark smell prey. When prey comes close, the wobbegong sucks the creature into its large mouth.

Shark Facts

SUPERORDER	Sharks
CLASS	Cartilaginous fish
SIZE	0.2–18.8 m (0.7–61.7 ft) long
RANGE	All oceans plus some rivers in the Americas, Africa, and Asia
DIET	Invertebrates, fish, birds, seals, dolphins, and turtles

Open Ocean

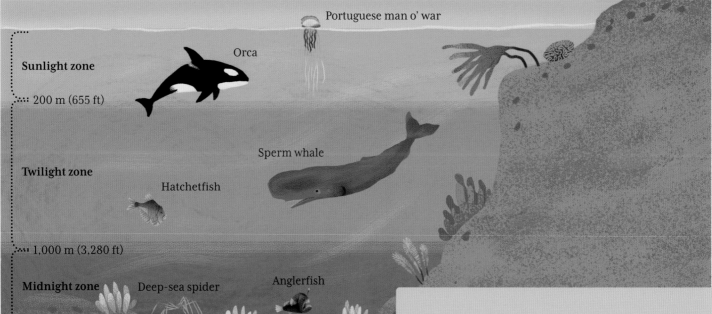

The orca, a toothed whale, swims in the ocean's sunlight zone, while the Portuguese man o' war, a relative of jellyfish, floats at the surface. The sperm whale and hatchetfish hunt in the twilight zone below. In the midnight zone, predators such as anglerfish and deep-sea spiders make their home.

The open ocean, also known as the pelagic (meaning "open sea" in ancient Greek) zone, is all ocean waters that are neither close to land nor the seafloor. The world's oceans, from largest to smallest, are the Pacific, Atlantic, Indian, Southern, and Arctic Oceans.

The Indian Ocean is the warmest ocean, its surface temperature between around 19 °C and 30 °C (66 °F and 86 °F), because it lies mostly in the tropical zone, which circles the equator. To the north and south of the tropical zone is the temperate zone, where cold water from the poles and warm water from the tropics mix together. The Arctic Ocean is the coldest ocean, as it is in the polar zone, where much of the water surface freezes in winter. Ocean animals are suited to a particular temperature range, with few able to move between tropical and polar waters.

Scientists also divide the open ocean into depth zones, based on how much light and warmth they receive from the Sun. From the surface to 200 m (655 ft) deep is the sunlight zone. Here, floating plants and algae can make their food from sunlight. They are food for plant-eaters, which are food for meat-eaters, making this the busiest pelagic zone. From 200 to 1,000 m (655 to 3,280 ft) is the twilight zone. A little sunlight reaches this deep, but it is not enough for plants and algae. At night, many twilight zone animals journey toward the surface to feed in the

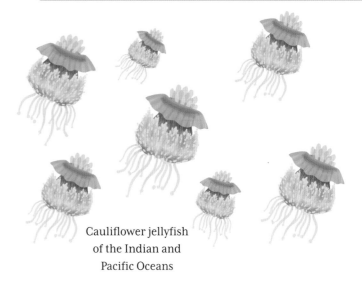

Cauliflower jellyfish of the Indian and Pacific Oceans

safety of darkness. From 1,000 m (3,280 ft) to the ocean floor, which reaches 10,929 m (35,856 ft), is the midnight zone. Here, it is always dark and cold, from 2 °C to 4 °C (36 °F to 39 °F). Animals feed on each other or on waste that drifts down from above. Some have special light-making organs that help them attract prey or a mate.

At a depth of 1,000 m (3,280 ft) in the tropical Atlantic Ocean, the dark water is around 2 °C (36 °F). There are few animals here, so the pelican eel has a wide mouth that can swallow prey much larger than the fish itself. To startle away this predator, the vampire squid pulls its arms over its head and gives a sudden flash of light. To attract prey, the black snaggletooth waves a glowing knob at the end of a finger-like chin extension called a barbel.

Indian Ocean

Up to 7,906 m (25,938 ft) deep, the Indian Ocean covers more than 70 million sq km (27 million sq miles). Its sunlit surface waters are busy with life, from tiny, floating plants, algae, and animals to large, predatory fish, mammals, and birds.

There are no hiding places in the sunlight zone of the open ocean. Most fish have a smoothly shaped body, so they can cut through the water quickly and cover large distances in their escape from predators. Many predators—including fish as well as mammals such as dolphins—are large and powerfully built to capture fast-moving prey.

Some predators, such as the ocean sunfish, are lone hunters, so they face less competition for food. Yet many open-ocean fish swim in large schools, gaining the advantage of having many eyes to watch for both prey and predators.

TROPICAL TWO-WING FLYING FISH

This fish can glide through the air to escape from predators. When pursued, it leaps out of the water for distances of up to 50 m (160 ft), with its large pectoral (side) fins acting a little like the wings of a plane.

INDO-PACIFIC SAILFISH

Up to 3 m (9.8 ft) long, this fish reaches 54 km/h (34 miles per hour) as it chases tuna and mackerel. It uses its long, sharp bill for hitting and slashing prey. When attacking, it raises its sail-like dorsal (back) fin, which helps prevent sideways movements of its head and bill.

SPINNER DOLPHIN

This dolphin is named for its habit of leaping out of the water, spinning and turning, then slapping back down onto the water. It may do this to slap parasites off its skin, to signal to other members of its group, or just for fun.

OCEAN SUNFISH

Weighing up to 2,000 kg (4,400 lb), this huge fish has an unusual body shape due to its lack of a tail fin. It takes its name from the long periods it spends basking on its side at the surface, where it soaks up the Sun's warmth before diving into deeper, colder water for prey.

GIANT OCEANIC MANTA RAY

This relative of sharks is up to 9 m (29.5 ft) long. It swims by flapping its wide, triangular pectoral fins. It feeds by swimming forward as it uses its cephalic (head) fins to funnel water containing small animals into its open mouth.

RED-FOOTED BOOBY

This seabird flies over the ocean in search of fish and squid that are feeding near the surface—then dives in at high speed. Air-filled sacs under the skin of its face help to cushion the blow as it hits the water surface.

Blue Whale

The largest animal ever to exist, the blue whale grows up to 29.9 m (98 ft) long. It weighs as much as 199 tons (219 US tons)—more than 16 African elephants. Like other whales, dolphins, and porpoises, the blue whale belongs to a group of mammals known as cetaceans.

SUITED TO WATER

Cetaceans are water-living mammals with a smoothly shaped body. They swim by swinging their tail up and down, while steering with their paddle-shaped front limbs. Cetaceans that are fast-moving hunters have a tall dorsal (back) fin to help with steering. Yet the blue whale has a very small dorsal fin, around 33 cm (1 ft) high, that has little use. Cetaceans also have a thick layer of fat, known as blubber, which keeps them warm.

Cetaceans are descended from four-legged, land-living mammals, but lost their back legs as they evolved to suit a life spent entirely in water. They give birth in the water to live babies, known as calves, which can swim immediately. Every 2 or 3 years, a female blue whale has a single calf, which is 6 to 7 m (20 to 23 ft) long.

Like all mammals, cetaceans must breathe air into their lungs, so they swim to the water surface regularly. They breathe through holes, known as blowholes, on top of their head. The blue whale has two blowholes, which spurt water and steam more than 12 m (49 ft) into the air when it breathes out. This whale is known to dive as deep as 315 m (1,033 ft) for up to 15 minutes at a time.

A blue whale calf stays with its mother for up for 7 months, drinking as much as 190 l (50 US gallons) of her milk each day. A blue whale may live for 80 to 90 years.

Bristles of baleen, up to 90 cm (3 ft) long, line the blue whale's upper jaw.

KRILL KILLER

Despite its great size, the blue whale is not a fierce hunter. It feeds almost entirely on tiny invertebrates called krill. When it finds a patch of krill, it swims quickly forward with its mouth open wide. Up to 220,000 l (58,000 US gallons) of water, filled with krill, surges into the whale's mouth. Its mouth has bristly comblike plates made of baleen. Baleen contains keratin, which is also found in human fingernails, bird beaks, and reptile scales. The krill are trapped by these plates, while the whale squeezes the water back out of its mouth.

Blue Whale Facts

SPECIES	*Balaenoptera musculus*
FAMILY	Rorqual whales
CLASS	Mammals
SIZE	21 to 29.9 m (69 to 98 ft) long
RANGE	All oceans, apart from ice-covered portions of the Arctic Ocean
DIET	Mostly krill, plus other small invertebrates and fish

Jellyfish

These brainless invertebrates have stinging tentacles that inject prey with venom. Adult jellyfish, named medusas, have a soft, umbrella-shaped body known as a bell. In the middle of the bell is the jellyfish's mouth. Adults swim by squeezing their bell, pushing water behind them.

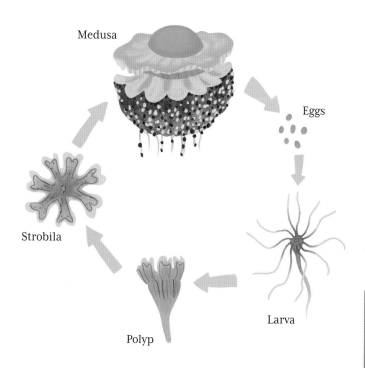

Medusa

Eggs

Strobila

Larva

Polyp

FRIED EGG JELLYFISH

Like other jellyfish, the fried egg has different body forms during its life. After hatching from its egg, it is a bean-shaped, swimming larva. The larva attaches to the seafloor, then turns into a stalk-shaped polyp, with upward-pointing tentacles. Plate-like segments grow then separate from the polyp, each one developing into a medusa.

ATOLLA JELLYFISH

Found in the deep, dark ocean, this jellyfish can make its own light, an ability known as bioluminescence. When the atolla is attacked, it gives a series of blue flashes, which not only startle the attacker but attract the attention of other predators that may attack the attacker.

WHITE-SPOTTED JELLYFISH

Unlike most of its relatives, this jellyfish does not have venom strong enough to harm prey. Instead, it has clusters of small mouthlets around the base of its frilly oral ("mouth") arms. As the jellyfish swims, water containing tiny creatures flows into the bell—and the mouthlets swallow the food.

LION'S MANE JELLYFISH

One of the largest jellyfish, the lion's mane has a bell more than 2 m (6.6 ft) wide. The bell has eight lobes, making it resemble an flower with eight petals. Each lobe has up to 150 tentacles, which trail behind the jellyfish to entangle fish and invertebrates.

CAULIFLOWER JELLYFISH

The cauliflower jellyfish's tentacles have stinging cells that inject some of the most powerful venom of any jellyfish. Each stinging cell houses a tiny needle-like stinger. When touched, the cell opens, letting water rush in. This makes the stinger shoot out, piercing prey and injecting the venom.

PURPLE-STRIPED JELLYFISH

This jellyfish has four frilly oral arms, as well as eight longer tentacles equipped with stinging cells. When the tentacles touch prey, they sting then bend toward the oral arms, passing them the stunned prey. An oral arm grasps the prey and squeezes it toward the mouth.

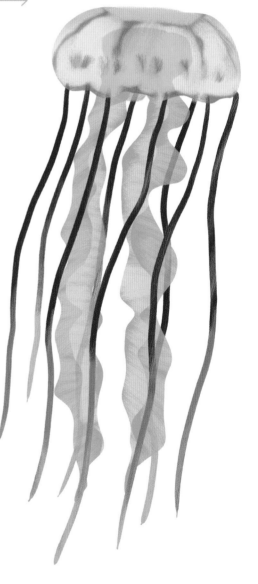

Jellyfish Facts

CLASS	True jellyfish
PHYLUM	Cnidarians
SIZE	0.05–36.6 m (0.16–120 ft) long
RANGE	All oceans as well as the brackish water of coastal lagoons and estuaries
DIET	Invertebrates, eggs, algae, and fish

Questions and Answers

WHAT ANIMAL CAN RUN THE FASTEST?

The cheetah, which lives in Africa and Iran, is the fastest land animal. Its light build, long legs, and muscular tail allow it to reach around 100 km/h (62 miles per hour) as it chases prey.

WHICH IS ANTARCTICA'S LARGEST LAND ANIMAL?

The largest fully land-living animal on the continent of Antarctica is a small, flightless insect known as the Antarctic midge. It is just 6 mm (0.2 in) long. The largest animal to spend part of its life on Antarctica is the southern elephant seal, which reaches 5.8 m (19 ft) in length and 4,000 kg (8,800 lb) in weight. It comes ashore only to rest or mate.

WHICH ANIMAL HAS THE THICKEST FUR?

The sea otter has the thickest fur, with up to 150,000 hairs per sq cm (970,000 per sq in). The fur has long, waterproof hairs, known as guard hairs, which keep dry a layer of short, soft underfur. The otter's fur keeps it warm in the coastal waters of the northern and eastern Pacific Ocean.

WHICH IS THE WORLD'S LARGEST ANIMAL?

The largest animal ever known to exist is the blue whale, which grows as big as 29.9 m (98 ft) long and weighs up to 199 tonnes (219 US tons)—more than 130 family cars. It can live for over 90 years.

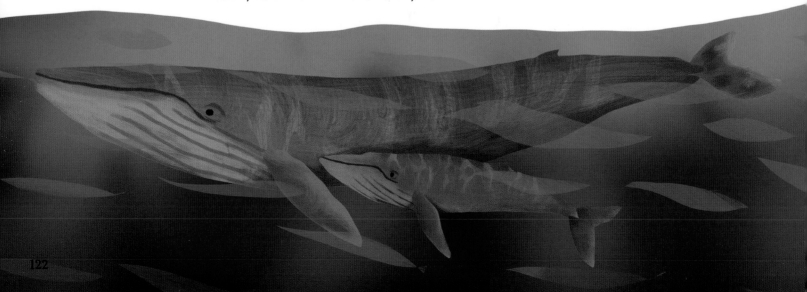

WHICH BIRD OF PREY IS THE LARGEST?

Found in South America's Andes Mountains, the Andean condor is the largest bird of prey. It weighs up to 15 kg (33 lb) and has a wingspan of up to 3.3 m (10.8 ft).

WHICH SCIENTIFIC ORDER OF ANIMALS CONTAINS THE MOST SPECIES?

The order of beetles, known as Coleoptera, contains the most known species: around 400,000. Beetles make up 40 percent of known insect species and 25 percent of known animal species. Since new species of beetles are discovered frequently, the number of known beetles is likely to rise.

WHICH SNAKE HAS THE MOST POWERFUL VENOM?

The inland taipan of central eastern Australia has the deadliest venom. One bite's worth of venom is enough to kill 100 adult men.

WHAT ANIMALS ARE MOST CLOSELY RELATED TO HUMANS?

Bonobos and chimpanzees are humans' closest living relatives. Like humans, these animals are in the great ape family of primates. The last shared ancestor of humans, bonobos, and chimpanzees lived somewhere between 4 million and 13 million years ago. After that time, humans began to evolve differently from bonobos and chimps.

WHICH IS THE TALLEST ANIMAL?

The tallest land animal is the giraffe, which reaches 5.7 m (18.7 ft) tall. Its long legs and neck allow it to reach leaves in high branches. One of the longest animals of all may be the lion's mane jellyfish, which has tentacles that trail for up to 36.6 m (120 ft).

WHAT ANIMAL HAS THE LONGEST TEETH?

The world's largest land animal, the African bush elephant, has the longest teeth. Its tusks, which are continuously growing teeth, can reach 3.5 m (11.5 ft) long and weigh 117 kg (258 lb).

Glossary

abdomen
In insects, the back part of the body; in vertebrates, the part of the body between the chest and hips.

air sac
An air-filled body part.

algae
Plantlike living things that usually live in and around water, such as seaweeds.

alpine zone
A treeless mountain region of low plants, below the snow line.

amphibian
An animal that usually spends part of its life on land and part in water, such as a frog.

antenna
A slender "feeler" found on the head of some invertebrates.

apex predator
A top predator in a habitat, without predators of its own.

arachnid
An invertebrate with eight legs and a body in two parts.

bacterium (plural: bacteria)
A tiny living thing with one cell.

bask
To warm up by resting in sunshine.

bioluminescent
Able to make its own light.

biome
A widespread community of plants and animals that are suited to their region's climate.

bird
An animal with a beak, wings, and feathers.

bird of prey
A bird that hunts animals that are large compared with its own size.

bog
A wetland, usually filled by rainwater, where dead plant material, known as peat, has built up.

boreal forest
A forest where most trees are coniferous; usually found in cold, northern regions.

brackish
A mixture of fresh and salty water.

broadleaf tree
A tree with flat leaves that produces seeds inside fruits.

camouflage
The way the pattern and shape of an animal make it less visible in its habitat.

canine
A pointed tooth between the front teeth (incisors) and back teeth (premolars) of a mammal.

canopy layer
The second highest layer of a rain forest, made up of the overlapping branches and leaves of trees.

carrion
The rotting flesh of dead animals.

cartilage
A strong bendy material found in the body.

cell
The smallest working part of a living thing's body.

class
A scientific group that includes animals with the same body plan, such as birds or mammals.

climate
The usual weather in a region over many years.

colony
A group of animals living together.

coniferous tree
A tree with needle-like or scale-like leaves that produces seeds in cones.

coral reef
An underwater structure made of the skeletons of millions of tiny animals called coral polyps.

deciduous tree
A tree that loses its leaves at the end of its growing season.

diapause
A period in an animal's life when activity and growth stops, usually during difficult weather conditions.

domestic
Tame and kept by humans.

dormant
When an animal enters a deep sleeplike state, with its body functions stopped or slowed.

drought
A long period without rainfall.

dry season
A regular period of dry weather.

emergent layer
The highest layer of a rain forest, made up of the tops of the tallest trees.

evergreen
A tree or other plant that keeps green leaves throughout the year.

evolve
To change gradually over time.

extinction
When a species dies out completely.

family
A group of species that are closely related, so that they look and behave much alike. For example, lions and tigers are in the cat family.

fen
A wetland, usually filled by groundwater, where dead plant material, known as peat, has built up.

fin
A body part that juts from the body of fish and some other water-living animals, helping them swim.

fish
A water-living animal, usually with fins, that takes oxygen from the water using gills.

forest
A wide area where many trees grow close together.

fresh water
Unsalted water, such as rivers, lakes, and ponds.

frost
A thin layer of ice that forms on the ground and objects when the temperature falls below freezing.

gill
An organ that takes oxygen from water.

gland
A body part that makes a substance for use in the body or for release.

glide
To fly through the air without flapping the wings.

global warming
Rising world temperatures caused mainly by human activities.

grassland
A wide area where most plants are grassses.

habitat
The natural home of an animal, plant, or other living thing.

hardy
Able to withstand harsh conditions.

hibernate
To spend the winter in a dormant, or resting, state.

hoof
A horny covering protecting the foot.

insect
An invertebrate with six legs and a three-part body: head, thorax, and abdomen.

insulation
A covering that keeps heat from escaping or entering.

intertidal zone
The area on the shore that is below water during high tides and above water when the sea draws out.

invertebrate
An animal without a backbone, such as a squid, spider, or insect.

larva (plural: larvae)
A young stage in the life cycle of some invertebrates, fish, and amphibians, during which the animal looks different from its adult form.

lichen
A living thing usually made up of algae and fungi growing together.

lung
An organ that takes oxygen from air.

mammal
An animal that grows hair at some point in its life and feeds its young on milk, such as a whale or human.

mangrove
A tree or shrub that usually lives in the intertidal zone.

marsh
A wetland where most plants are low grasses, rushes, and reeds.

metamorphosis
The change in body shape that most amphibians and some invertebrates and fish go through as they grow into adults.

migrate
To move from one region to another at particular times of year.

montane zone
A region on a mountain's slopes that is often forested.

moorland
An area of poor soil where most plants are tough, low grasses and shrubs.

nectar
A sugary liquid made by flowers.

nocturnal
Active at night.

nutrient
A substance needed by an animal's body for growth and health.

order
A group of families that are closely related. For example, the cat and dog families are in the meat-eating Carnivora order.

organ
A body part that does a particular job, such as the heart or brain.

oxygen
A gas found in air and water that is needed by animals' cells for energy.

parasite
A living thing that lives in, on, or around another living thing, taking food and other benefits from it.

permafrost
In regions close to the poles, a below-surface layer of soil that remains frozen all year.

plant
A living thing that makes its own food from sunlight.

plumage
A bird's covering of feathers.

polar
In the areas close to the poles, where it is very cold all year.

pollen
A powder made by flowers. It can fertilize other flowers of the same species, so they make seeds.

predator
An animal that hunts other animals.

prey
An animal that is killed by another animal for food.

pupa
A stage in the life of an insect when it is changing from larva to adult.

range
The area where an animal is found.

reptile
An animal with a dry skin, covered in scales, that usually lays eggs on land.

roost
To rest or sleep.

sap
A sweet liquid that circulates inside plants.

scale
A small, hard plate that protects the skin of most fish and reptiles.

sea ice
Ice that forms on the surface of the ocean.

sea level
The height of the sea's surface.

seed
A small object produced by a plant from which a new plant can grow.

shrub
A plant, with several woody stems, that is usually shorter than a tree.

snout
The nose and mouth of an animal.

species
A group of living things that look similar and can mate together.

subspecies
A population of a species that lives in a particular area and differs from other populations of the species.

subtidal zone
The area on the shore that is always below water.

swamp
A wetland where most plants are trees.

tadpole
The larva of an amphibian.

taiga
A forest where most trees are coniferous; usually found in cold, northern regions.

temperate
In the areas between the tropics and polar regions, where it is neither very hot nor very cold.

tentacle
A long, thin body part, used for feeling or grabbing.

tide
The rising and falling of the ocean at the shore, caused by the pull of the Moon's gravity on the water.

tree
A plant with a thick, woody stem, known as a trunk.

tropical
In the area around the equator, where it is very hot all year.

tundra
A cold, treeless region.

understory layer
The second lowest layer of a rain forest, made up of shrubs and other low plants.

venom
A poison made by an animal.

vertebrate
An animal with a backbone: a fish, amphibian, reptile, bird, or mammal.

webbed feet
Having toes that are linked by tissue and skin, making them paddle-like.

wetland
Land that is covered by water either throughout the year or during particular seasons.

wet season
A regular period of rainy weather.

woodland
An area where many trees grow but sunlight reaches the ground between them.